"It's time to trade in the lie of being left out for the truth that there's a place where you were made to belong! Don't know how to get from here to there? Kristen is the kind of guide who will pick you up with coffee in one hand and a bouquet of real, honest stories in the other and drive you there in person, with music and laughter blaring all the way. This book is your instant invitation to belonging. All you have to do is accept it."

Lisa-Jo Baker, bestselling author of *Never Unfriended* and *Surprised by Motherhood*

"This book is an invitation to sit on a front porch swing with Kristen Strong— a woman who truly knows how to encourage and who understands what it's like to feel alone and finally find your heart's real home. I've considered Kristen a dear friend for years, and now I'll also think of her as my wise and help-ful 'Belonging Mentor.' Take a seat, turn to the first page, and you will too."

Holley Gerth, bestselling author of *You're Already Amazing* and *Fiercehearted*

"Maybe this sounds like you: you're on the isolating back roads of life—miles away from where you want to be—and feeling like you'll never find your way, *like you'll never really belong.* Along comes our friend Kristen, who deeply understand the struggle you face. She is a trusted companion who will point you to the One who is on those back roads with you. This book contains unforgettable lessons on belonging as well as specific action steps to help you find peace on days when it seems like you're all alone. Don't miss this book!"

Jennifer Dukes Lee, author of *It's All Under Control* and *The Happiness Dare*

"*Back Roads to Belonging* is a gentle, walk-beside-you companion for those longing for community and connection. The phrase 'back roads' says it all. This is no strident, finger-wagging book. This isn't a book of instant solu-tions. It is a loving message from a friend who has been there and back again and speaks to us in a voice that is folksy and friendly, wise and warm. Now I understand that back roads, though they require patience, attentiveness, and a willingness to walk a quieter way, also offer beautiful views and intimate encounters. Kristen shares her own hard-earned wisdom and the wisdom of many others in order to remind us that no matter how far we wander, we can never wander outside of God's love."

Christie Purifoy, author of *Roots and Sky* and *Placemaker*

"Kristen's generous voice, using storytelling that is both hilarious and poi-gnant, offers us the comfy cushion on the couch and the best throw pillow to hug against our fluffy spots as she scooches over to make room for our fears, our insecurities, and our 'we don't belong' feelings, and then she leans in close and whispers in the pages, 'Belonging is woven into our being.' It is a gift for us all, nothing asked, nothing earned. *Back Roads to Belonging* invites us to explore those woven places with Kristen, a trusted companion, who's picked at the threads herself and discovered a God who's stitched a masterpiece in each one of us and called us beloved."

Alia Joy, author of *Glorious Weakness*

"We were created to belong, yet so many of us feel like we don't. On the outside looking in, we hold on to a hidden ache, wondering what defect we have that keeps us from being invited in. Our only option is to try harder, offer more, do whatever it takes. Or perhaps stop trying, stop caring, stop feeling. But what if there is another option? Kristen Strong shows us there is! Filled with stories we can relate to and powerful truths we need, *Back Roads to Belonging* shows us an uncommon path that leads to the place where we *already* belong."

Renee Swope, bestselling author of *A Confident Heart* and former radio cohost for Proverbs 31 Ministries

"Kristen's book is a wonderful testimony to the power of belonging. In a time when so many are held back by uncertainty, wrestle with insecurity, and are confused about their identity and calling, this book provides a needed—and deeply practical—path forward: rest and contentment in Jesus. Kristen's words are deep and brimming with honesty, humor, and a realness that you'll love and relate to. I found myself refreshed, challenged, and inspired."

Dominic Done, author of *When Faith Fails: Finding God in the Shadow of Doubt*

"Who hasn't wondered, Do I belong here? And who hasn't staked her entire identity on the answer to that question? In *Back Roads to Belonging*, Kristen vulnerably tells her own stories of feeling *out* and finding her way *in* . . . but maybe not in the exact ways you'd think. Kristen shows us the view from the 'back roads,' which require us to first belong to ourselves and to God before we will ever experience belonging with others. Finding our seat at the table is fulfilling, to be sure, and Kristen beautifully reminds us that our chair was there all along."

Leeana Tankersley, author of *Begin Again*

"Our hearts ache for a place to belong, yet so often our fears and insecurities keep us from the journey God intends. With biblical insight and practical encouragement, Kristen's grace-filled and powerful storytelling compels us to take the slow route to our own place of genuine belonging. The more I read *Back Roads to Belonging*, the more I want to find that place. Definitely a recommended read."

Jen Schmidt, speaker, host of the Becoming Conference, author of *Just Open the Door*, and founder of the *Balancing Beauty and Bedlam* blog

back roads to Belonging

Unexpected Paths to Finding Your Place and Your People

Kristen Strong

Revell

a division of Baker Publishing Group
Grand Rapids, Michigan

Published by Revell
a division of Baker Publishing Group
PO Box 6287, Grand Rapids, MI 49516-6287
www.revellbooks.com

Printed in the United States of America

Library of Congress Cataloging-in-Publication Data is on file at the Library of Congress, Washington, DC.

ISBN 978-0-8007-3552-4

Unless otherwise indicated, Scripture quotations are from The Holy Bible, English Standard Version® (ESV®), copyright © 2001 by Crossway, a publishing ministry of Good News Publishers. Used by permission. All rights reserved. ESV Text Edition: 2016

Scripture quotations labeled CSB are from the Christian Standard Bible®, copyright © 2017 by Holman Bible Publishers. Used by permission. Christian Standard Bible® and CSB® are federally registered trademarks of Holman Bible Publishers.

Scripture quotations labeled GNT are from the Good News Translation in Today's English Version-Second Edition. Copyright © 1992 by American Bible Society. Used by permission.

Scripture quotations labeled KJV are from the King James Version of the Bible.

Scripture quotations labeled Message are from THE MESSAGE, copyright © 1993, 1994, 1995, 1996, 2000, 2001, 2002 by Eugene H. Peterson. Used by permission of NavPress. All rights reserved. Represented by Tyndale House Publishers, Inc.

Scripture quotations labeled NASB are from the New American Standard Bible® (NASB), copyright © 1960, 1962, 1963, 1968, 1971, 1972, 1973, 1975, 1977, 1995 by The Lockman Foundation. Used by permission. www.Lockman.org

Scripture quotations labeled NIV are from the Holy Bible, New International Version®. NIV®. Copyright © 1973, 1978, 1984, 2011 by Biblica, Inc.™ Used by permission of Zondervan. All rights reserved worldwide. www.zondervan.com. The "NIV" and "New International Version" are trademarks registered in the United States Patent and Trademark Office by Biblica, Inc.™

Scripture quotations labeled NKJV are from the New King James Version®. Copyright © 1982 by Thomas Nelson. Used by permission. All rights reserved.

Scripture quotations labeled NLT are from the Holy Bible, New Living Translation, copyright © 1996, 2004, 2007, 2013, 2015 by Tyndale House Foundation. Used by permission of Tyndale House Publishers, Inc., Carol Stream, Illinois 60188. All rights reserved.

Scripture quotations labeled TLB are from The Living Bible, copyright © 1971. Used by permission of Tyndale House Publishers, Inc., Carol Stream, Illinois 60188. All rights reserved.

Some names and details have been changed to protect the privacy of the individuals involved.

19 20 21 22 23 24 25   7 6 5 4 3 2 1

To two of the dearest, kindest men:
my daddy, James Hoyd O'Neill,
and my father-in-law, Dan Strong.
Thank you for your real-deal examples
of welcoming others in.

Contents

Foreword

I SPEND A LOT OF TIME looking out my living room windows and into the street. On any given day, I see kids trudging to school, mamas pushing strollers and pulling wagons piled high with laundry, businessmen in slacks conducting "walking meetings," joggers, night-shifters, and preschoolers riding tricycles. There are also the black squirrels, the stray cats, the cars driving too fast, and the maple trees reminding us to slow down.

I never imagined my life here.

My family arrived six years ago, fresh off the farm. I thought I was made for wildflowers, open fields, wraparound porches, and tomato vines. That was my comfort level, my preference. It was where I belonged. But life will do what it does, won't it? It'll take us by surprise.

The early days in this painfully ordinary, well-loved (read: slightly shabby) neighborhood were a crash course on surrender. I didn't know a soul and my comfort zone was but a memory. Everything was unfamiliar and more than a little uncertain. I knew there was purpose in this flash life-change and though there were butterflies and even a few sparrows flapping in my stomach, I was excited.

I was also lonely.

We moved into the neighborhood with no agenda other than to love and be loved by the people around us, a ruckus of contrast and extremes. The abundant life we were promised wasn't just about bright spots and blue skies after all. There was sadness mixed in. We

9

had to take risks and learn to listen. Through the emotional rigors of everyday life, even a classic introvert like me needed the support of true community. I knew it was true, but I was nervous. Awkward. I didn't know where to start or if I would ever fit in.

It doesn't matter where we live, how long we've been there, or how long we plan to stay. We will all face a crisis of belonging, eventually. Offering the backup we need, *Back Roads to Belonging* is a kindhearted field guide through the lowlands of longing. Kristen, our generous companion, is someone you'll want to keep near even after you've found your way.

Each page that follows is a seat at the table, an invitation toward humility, and permission to burn the bootstraps that have kept us believing we're fine on our own. (If we're honest, we'd rather wear sneakers anyway.) A woman whose life detours have taught her the strength of sweetness and the power of grit, Kristen is wise in the ways of roots and new growth. "We don't see what the poppies and peonies do below ground," she writes, "but we have faith that something is going on."

Belonging takes time. It requires extra helpings of patience and compassion, both for ourselves and for others. As it turns out, I was made for wildflowers that pop up through the cracks of busted sidewalks. I've learned to love alleys and to be attentive to the life happening on our tiny front stoop. As for the tomato vines? They don't care where they're planted as long as they can see the sun.

Building community is taxing, but the work is worth it. We were never meant to go it alone. The world is waiting for us to show up and receive our belonging place. Holding the hope of Christ like a flashlight in the dead of night, Kristen takes our hand and walks us into truth. You belong. You are brave enough to go first. You are faithful enough to try again.

Deep breaths.
First steps.
Let's go.

Shannan Martin, bestselling author
of *The Ministry of Ordinary Places* and *Falling Free*

Acknowledgments

No BOOK GETS WRITTEN without a posse of support, and this one is no exception!

Thank you, God, for all the ways you give abundantly and love extravagantly.

Thank you, Jesus, for your saving work that brought all of us from the outside in.

David, thank you for asking me to marry you twenty-four years ago. You are my safest place, and you'll always be my favorite person with whom I belong.

James, Ethan, and Faith, you three are such delights! Thank you for introducing me to the best shows, for joining me in my enthusiasm over the little things, and for teaching me over and over how my richest belonging place is home with you and your dad.

My family, especially Mom, Sara, Megan, and Bev; thank you for your support and love. I love you!

My wingwomen Aimée, Allison, Cheryl, Connie, Elizabeth, Holley, JDL, Kim, Lisa-Jo, Maria, Rebecca, Renee, and Selena; thank you for your prayers and friendship—they give me confidence and joy.

Aimée, thank you for letting me ask all the insecure questions and for answering them with shoot-from-the-hip honesty yet wild-and-fierce kindness. Your friendship is one of my favorite things.

To Village Seven and especially Cornerstone Community; you don't know how many churches we visited before finding a home within your doors. Thank you for your kindness.

Ruth Samsel, you've mentored me in a dozen ways, only one of which was as an author. Thank you for your generosity and love. I'll adore you always. Teresa Evenson, thank you for being one stellar advocate. Your presence and voice have been such gifts!

Kaitlyn, thank you for knowing everything about everything. What would I do without you?

To Shannan, your long'n' lean self is chockful of robust writing talent. Thank you for doing me the extravagant honor of writing this book's foreword and for being one of my favorite belong-makers.

To Andrea Doering; thank you for giving me this opportunity once again—love you so!

To my editor Michelle Rapkin and the entire team at Revell, including Lindsey Spoolstra, Patti Brinks, Wendy Wetzel, and Brianne Dekker; thank you for partnering with me and helping me send this book out and about in such great shape!

To Lindsey; thank you for being the extra brain I needed. You're a wonder!

To Holley, Alli, Connie, Aundrea, Kelli, Michelle, Emmy, Chelsea, Lauren, Rebecca, and Salena; thank you for generously sharing your stories within this book's pages. Doing so was no small thing but a very brave thing. Your contributions have made all the difference.

To my (in)courage writer-friends; you are effervescent lights who do a bang-up job of welcoming women in. Thank you for doing the same for me.

To my porch friends and blog readers; thank you for being my people, and thank you for making a wide open space for me.

Introduction

From the get-go, here, I'm going to spell out for you one of my greatest fears in life. And I don't believe I'm the only one who has struggled with this fear, either. Perhaps it has also followed you around far too long in far too bossy a way.

This fear is not that my kids will be kidnapped. (I've feared that before, certainly, but given that two of them are inches upon inches taller than me and the other is saturated in jalapeño-hot sassiness, I don't fear that so much these days.)

It's not that I'll lose my husband. (We're both going to go eventually, I know.)

It's not that age will hit me with facial wrinkles, wiry gray hair, and chronic lower-back pain. (That's already happening, and I'm rolling with it via more than a little help from the Ulta beauty counter, my hair gal Lindsey, and yoga here and there.)

Honestly, these things don't spend a lot of time lounging in my thoughts. But here is one thing that *has* wandered through my mind all too often: the fear of not belonging, of feeling *I don't belong where I want to belong, and I'm forever meant to be on the outside looking in.*

Maybe this has been an issue for you as well.

Wherever my current "outside" is, I imagine it as a house I'm standing near. I approach its front windows and cup my hands on the cool glass—or on the computer screen or phone snapshot—and take in a scene I'd love to wander into myself: women talking in warm, cozy groups, eyes bright with plans in the making or dreams come true. Sometimes I see this, turn the right way, and say, *Thank you, God, for giving them this gift.* But all too often I turn the wrong way and say, *Why, God, can't you give me this gift?*

Then I'll begin to answer my own question. I'll tell myself it's because I'm either too much or not enough, depending on the situation.

A favorite novel of mine is *Pride and Prejudice,* and there is a scene played out in movie adaptations of the book that sums up this feeling quite well. In the one I watch the most (the Keira Knightley version, not the BBC one), Elizabeth "Lizzie" Bennett, the story's protagonist, has just met Mr. Darcy, the very wealthy, well-connected aristocrat who's the other central character of the story. Lizzie overhears Mr. Darcy discussing her with his friend Mr. Bingley. When Mr. Bingley comments to Mr. Darcy that Elizabeth is very agreeable, Mr. Darcy arrogantly replies, "Perfectly tolerable, I daresay. But not handsome enough to tempt me."[1]

While Lizzie takes this stinging criticism with relatively good humor, I wince every time I watch this scene. I wince partly because Lizzie overhears him say it. But mostly I cringe because similar words are far too familiar to me—except I'm the one who says them about myself. *Kristen, you may be perfectly tolerable, but you're not _____ enough for this event or that group of people.* If Mr. Darcy had said that about me, on some level I would have agreed (after my defensive streak threatened to clobber him).

But on the other hand, I want to convince you I *am* worth your time. I want to get your attention by inserting myself into your conversation. I want to politely but firmly move my way to the front of the room. I want to be noticed and appreciated for what I can offer and contribute.

As a woman who's walked this earth for over forty years now, I can tell you I've brushed against this feeling of being on the outside and all it encompasses more than I want to admit, especially throughout my years as a military wife. During that time, my family would move to a new location every three years or so, and I would become reacquainted with the overwhelming realization of having no sense of belonging. I repeatedly maneuvered the awkwardness that comes with being an outsider, and I resented the amount of time and just plain *work* it took to become accepted, appreciated, and *in*.

Flipping through individual memories from those years, I stop to consider a few that stand out in distinctly vibrant colors. When I was a young mom living in New Mexico, I joined a moms' group comprised of women from all over our new town. A few weeks after joining, I invited several moms and their kids over for a "playdate lunch." I spent much time crafting peanut butter and jelly cut-out sandwiches and fruit salad. For the grown-ups, I fixed chicken and mandarin orange salad. I baked chocolate chip cookies. I brought down more toys, including extra LEGOs and Lincoln Logs from the boys' top closet shelf, so all the kids would have plenty of options for play. And then I sat and waited as *not one single person* came to my house.

I'm not sure I've ever felt more like a big, dumb loser.

Fast-forward a few years, when my family lived in the Midwest, and I was then in a season of parenting three tiny humans instead of two. We attended a church full of beautifully kind and loving people, and after some time I (finally) began forming relationships with a few of the good folks there. On one particular Sunday, my husband was out of town because of work. I managed to get all three of my little ones to church and Sunday school as well as remember to bring my dish of garlic mashed potatoes for the potluck picnic after the service.

I enjoyed the potluck immensely, downing long swigs of conversation with other grown-ups like I hadn't had any in a while. (Because I hadn't.) The kids and I gobbled up our buffet lunch of deliciousness, and not long after, my daughter needed to use the restroom. Once we took care of business and returned to the picnic area, I looked around to see my table empty. Scanning the lawn, I noticed all the remaining picnic-goers—many of them longtime members of our church—sitting in a big circle, all laughing and talking like only a day with warm sunshine and longtime relationships encourages.

Clear as church bells, I remember staring at that circle of people while my kids ran in circles around me. I sighed and said, "What does one have to *do* to really feel like she belongs, anyhow?"

I plopped down in a chair near my empty table and pretended to be occupied with the contents of my daughter's diaper bag. Soon afterward, I wrangled my kids into the minivan and headed home.

You may be thinking, *Kristen, why didn't you go up to that circle of people and ask if you could join them?* I probably should've. Looking back on that now, I'm certain they would have welcomed me into the circle. But at the time, I remember seeing that cozy, connected group and realizing I didn't share their history or stories. I believed that without a direct invite, inserting myself into their circle felt at best awkward and presumptuous, and at worst like a massive intrusion.

Because we had attended that church for a while and I had begun to connect with people, I thought I belonged. Instead, that circle of chairs reminded me that I wasn't really *in* like I thought, and maybe I didn't deserve to belong like I wanted.

I was reflecting on this the other day as I walked past my sons' room and overheard a conversation they were having with a friend of theirs. That friend, upon hearing I was a published author, said to my sons, "That's so cool! Does your mom know any famous people?"

Quick as a wink, one son answered, "Nah, not really. But I think she knows people who know people."

Throwing my hand over my mouth, I speed-walked to my room and laughed my head off, all while thinking to myself, *Yep, son, that about nails it.*

Writing a book doesn't mean I'm in with famous people. Or even you-and-I regular people, for that matter. I'm a new author most people have never heard of. In the same way, making a connection with a person or two doesn't mean you or I are suddenly in at church or the in-laws' dinner table, or with the moms' group, the gang from work, or the PTA.

Perhaps, like me, you thought that once this or that happened you'd move *in* more, but in reality you weren't as in as you thought. Sometimes I can laugh about this, but I've certainly been known to cry instead, believing all over again I'm out, out, out.

And when that happens, I've also scolded myself for spending too much time at the corner of Crybaby and Feels-Sorry-for-Herself. After all, I have a good, good life with a great husband and three healthy, hilarious children, and I get to do work I love to pieces. All that is 100 percent true. But what's also true is that I can be thankful for every bit of these gifts *and* still be unsure of how and where I belong in other important areas of my life.

If we're the newcomer to the neighborhood, the newest congregant at our church, or just can't figure out how to connect with our coworkers, we can absolutely be thankful for the goodness of God yet still struggle with our sense of belonging in those places.

• • •

We want that belonging to be *a real thing already*, and instead it's an excursion, one that asks us to take the slow route to our place of genuine belonging. For those struggling to fit in, our very specific and creative God asks us to abandon the loud boulevard of attention-demanding behaviors for the byways of remaining in Christ and relaxing into the unique role he has for each of us. Not so we can isolate ourselves in a country hideaway. Rather, the back road way is being attentive to God's direction as to how we can create an environment of connection in a culture of disconnection—no matter where we live. It's the way rooted in breathe-easy sincerity and refreshing authenticity. The back road way may take a little longer to get to our destination, but it's worth the trip.

Ironically, once we slow down to accept this, we arrive at our destination faster.

Sometimes, being *out* is genuine, not just something we've twisted into truth inside our heads. But whether we hold proof of being on the outside or simply perceive it as fact, the lonely feelings it brings are

17

very real. At the heart of the matter, we fear we don't belong because something is intrinsically wrong with us. We're *too this* or *not enough that* to find our place where we're welcomed as we are for who we are.

Regardless of why we feel out rather than in, it's hard for this not to influence the way we move about in our families, homes, communities, and lives.

Maybe you're a mama who feels she's on the outside of the booster club at your kids' school. Maybe you're a daughter who dared to go against the family mantra and is now outside the once-upon-a-time welcoming circle of home. Maybe you're an empty nester who fears she's now on the outside of her children's lives. Or the retiree who believes she's outlived her usefulness and is on the outside of all those young'uns around her.

You and me, we don't want to feel like we don't belong. So what can we do to not feel that way?

First of all, we can know that Jesus totally understands this and considers it a valid feeling, not a crybaby move. From his birth outside the inn, Jesus experienced what it was like to be on the outside. Yet he still lived as one very much accepted, because he was accepted by his Father. He didn't worry about being on the outside looking in. He was on the outside looking up.

The same is true for us. We are accepted and adored by God right here, right now. We deserve to belong because it's woven into our being; it's the way God made us. And he wants to walk alongside us down the meandering back road way as we feel and know our own sense of belonging. By the time you finish reading this book, I pray you're able to own a stronger sense of this acceptance and belonging in your heart and life.

Second, if we want to feel that we belong, we need to know that being in is not something to achieve but something to receive. It is first receiving the truth that God does not dish out leftovers to any of us. Psalm 33:5 states that the earth is drenched in God's affectionate satisfaction. Drenched, it says. And no Bible translation is going to include a clause stating *except for* _____ with your name at the end.

We're each under the shower of blessings, and we're not left out to dry. Grasping this truth is also grasping the contented life no matter where we are and in what circles we move—or don't move.

I would never promise that, after you read this book, you'll never ever again struggle to know you truly belong. Rather, I believe this book will be a song for your heart and soul, a regular tune to come back to whose melody points you toward your Father in heaven who gives good gifts, including a sense of belonging. As you travel your own back road to belonging, I believe this book's steady beat will be a compass bringing your heart back to its true North.

Hear me sing the song's chorus to you now.

Yes, you belong.

Yes, you belong.

Yes, you belong.

Because Jesus came for you, you're already in, in every way that counts.

May we gather hope and belief as we travel the back roads to belonging together.

Part I

Wandering

Wandering isn't pointless.
It is a positive step in finding your
place and your people.

one

Sitting Out

The truth is we often wait for clarity. But God wants us to confide in Him about the actual journey—and how we're doing on it—more than about getting to the destination.

Bonnie Gray, *Whispers of Rest*

I MARCHED RIGHT OUT of that gathering room and down the short hall and swung open the bathroom door. I made a beeline for the nearest stall, slammed its door shut, then kicked it with all the might my size 10 cowboy boots could muster.

And then I kicked it again, enjoying the satisfaction found in rattling the heavy metal door.

Yes, I suppose it wasn't a particularly dignified thing to do, but I didn't care. I don't remember if there were others in the bathroom with me. To borrow a phrase of my daddy's, I was as mad as a wet hornet, and I didn't give a lick about appearances. In that moment my anger came out in the best way I knew to express it.

What caused my bathroom fit? Well, let me backtrack a bit.

At one point along my journey as wife to a man in the United States Air Force, I found myself in the eighty-third situation (give or take; I never exaggerate) of being the newish girl in town. Within that town, we had been attending a church for over a year. In my mind, we were well past the point when acquaintances should stop being acquaintances and start being friends. I walked into our church for an evening function and scanned the familiar room looking for someone with whom I could converse. While I'd been with these good folks many times before, I was still new enough that I didn't yet know everyone in the large group. As my eyes swept from one end of the room to the other, I noticed everyone was huddled in pairs or trios, talking intently with one another. So I plopped down in the seat nearest me and placed my purse beside my chair.

I scanned again, looking for a comfortable break in a cluster where I could easily and nonchalantly saunter over and say hello. Coming up empty, I wrung my hands, one over the other, like I was washing them without soap and water.

Like I was trying to wash out that nervous feeling creeping up in my heart.

After some time, with no conversation appearing approachable, I walked over to the dessert table, picked up a napkin and a plastic plate, and placed a hearty slice of lemon cake on it. I went back to my seat to eat the cake, thankful I had something in my hands on which to focus. With every bite, I glanced up to see if I could make eye contact with anyone, but I couldn't.

I've been here before—more than once. And while time has taught me how to handle being a wallflower just fine, this time it got to me. So I stood up and walked calmly but purposely out of the meeting room to the bathroom, where I let my frustration and just plain sadness have their way.

After kicking the door, I crossed my arms and said, "Why can't I just enjoy myself here and not feel like the loser at the party? When will I know I belong?"

I cried like a woman who was heart-weary from the work that getting to know people entails. I cried like a woman tired from all the effort repeatedly invested in finding my place. I was certain that by the time I started to feel like I belonged, it would be time for our family to move once again.

I do understand that being in these situations from time to time is not exactly newsworthy. It's just a part of life, really. But if you're someone like me, who's had to do it over and over again, well, you know it's just plain exhausting and more than a little disheartening.

The crux of the problem for me was this: I thought more than enough time had passed for me to have gained a sense of belonging within this community. However, I couldn't seem to get anyone else on board with this.

In other words, the way things *were* messed up the way things were *supposed to be.*

• • •

You probably have your own I-wish-I-could-belong-here story too. Whether in the past or present (or both), you may have been placed in communities that didn't fit well, or maybe even in a home that wasn't warm, accepting, or inviting. You wonder if you'll always be on the fringes of acceptance and never own a sense of place. You feel separated and resentful, believing your undesirable "right now" is the best thing you have going for you.

When this happens to me, it's like I'm in the middle of a softball game but am perennially banished to the dugout, where I sit eating peanuts and tossing their shells. I want to play, but my team is doing well enough without me, so I warm the bench.

While it's perfectly healthy to acknowledge these feelings rather than act like they're not there, it's also good to acknowledge the hope found in the fact that God never intended for us to feel this way. He doesn't see you and me as sitting on the outside, and he doesn't want us to see ourselves in that light either. We belong in his "home country" of the "kingdom of faith" (Eph. 2:19 Message). As a result, you and I are never in the margin of God's best for us but in the middle. So, if something doesn't fit within our communities, it's more likely either it isn't supposed to or it doesn't fit *yet*.

Having actually been a subpar softball player who spent her fair share of time on the bench, I can look at that scenario with grown-up eyes and see it within its proper context. Either I didn't play much because the coach knew more about what was best for the team, or softball just wasn't my game. And I can't begin to tell you the degree to which softball wasn't mine. I come from a family that's neck-deep in sports talent, and I got approximately 0 percent of it. While I'm now okay with having different skills and talents, there was a period of time in my young life when I wanted nothing more than to be able to pitch or catch a fly ball like my sisters. I'd have given away my Cabbage Patch doll to hit a line drive like one of my cousins—or hit the ball at all, really. Alas, my best work on the field was praying the ball never came to me so I wouldn't have to figure out what to do with it when it did.

What I'm saying here is softball—or any sport, really—just ain't my game.

It's the same when considering our belongingness, I think. God knows the big picture, and he may be asking each of us to give more time for our sense of place to develop. Or it's possible he has in mind for us to take another path toward our place of belonging. Because sometimes we have to first try something that doesn't fit in order to find the thing that *does*.

It saddens me to no end that many people, overwhelmed by hopelessness, give up before they get that experience of the right fit within their communities. And within that group, many permanently give in to hopelessness. According to the CDC, the suicide rate in our country is up 30 percent since 1999. While that rate is up among both men and women, in all racial and ethnic groups, and across all neighborhoods, middle-aged adults had the largest number of suicides and the highest increase in suicide rates.[1]

Not long ago, my adopted town of Colorado Springs had the singular distinction of being both one of the top five places to live in the United States and a place with one of the nation's worst suicide rates.[2] While attending a suicide awareness program put on by my kids' school district, I discovered that in Colorado, one in fourteen students attempt suicide. That would be unfathomable to me if it weren't for the fact that kids at my own children's high school and youth group were among those lost.

There are several factors that come into play with suicide—difficulty in getting quality mental health care and the legitimate contagion factor, to name two—but research tells us that while counseling, a good diet, and other aids can help, another important way to combat suicidal thoughts is to have a strong sense of belonging, a place, and a people.[3]

The world tells us we have everything we need within us to overcome any obstacle, reach any dream, and soar any skyline. But eventually, you and I are going to come to the end of ourselves. We're going to realize we don't have what it takes on our own—because we don't. Eventually, we'll land smack-dab in the middle of our limitations and discover our own variety of banged-up disappointments and unforeseen hardships. If I'm the beginning and end of all available "bootstrap" strength, then I'm in a rather hopeless state indeed.

This is where we see the hope found in our heavenly Father and his Son Jesus highlighted like a comet shooting across the ebony-black sky. We have this hope as "a strong and trustworthy anchor for our souls" (Heb. 6:19 NLT). And that Hope walks with us in this sin-muddied, difficult life. It doesn't matter what circumstances land in our lap. We have infinite hope because we have an infinite God who is just getting started at "impossible."

You think you're the exception to the rule and you'll never belong? Not true. He may ask you and me to sit out for an inning or a game, but he doesn't ask us to sit out on life altogether. It doesn't matter how others have treated us, because only God's opinion of us counts. He absolutely desires each of us to have a place of belonging, but it may require a good bit of wandering to reach it.

• • •

When I'm trying to participate in something that doesn't yet fit, can I consider sitting out as an opportunity to discern if I'm holding my desire to belong in a specific group or location in a higher place than I should? Is sitting out an opportunity to discover if being *out* of this group means God wants me in another? Or if he wants me to know I'm *in* in another way? It's well worth our time to consider sitting out as a back road way to finding our place of belonging. It just might be the gift that allows you and me the opportunity to evaluate our position within where we want to belong and where God calls us to belong.

Back in that bathroom, this is exactly what I sought to do: evaluate my position. And it occurred to me that just as I can offer myself as a willing participant within a group, I can't demand they accept my offer. Just as Jesus doesn't demand we accept his presence in our lives, we rest knowing that extending the offer is where the back road blessings are. In walking with God along the slower-paced back road way, we begin to see how to involve him within our everyday lives—and we also see how he's already involved.

So on that evening sitting in the bathroom, I remembered that within the large gathering room I did not move alone. I breathed deeply enough to raise my shoulders and my confidence. I left that stall, walked to the sink to wash my hands, and gave myself a quick pep talk in the mirror. I calmly but deliberately walked out of the bathroom and into the meeting room toward a duo of ladies in conversation. Sitting myself down beside them, I said, "How's your day going, girls?"

They answered with kind eyes and inviting conversation, no furrowed brows or *who invited you?* stares. So I tossed my expectations over my shoulder and instead offered them the opportunity to take my hand of friendship.

Whether they took it or not, I refused the temptation to get off the path toward finding my place of belonging. I breathed in and out and silently repeated these words like a prayer: *I will be where Christ wants me in this moment.*

May you and I stay on the back road that invites us to remember we are never pushed out of our home country of the kingdom of faith. While we may spend time sitting out, that time spent won't be wasted. It's just a necessary part of finding our place and our people.

We are in the center of God's plans for us, our forever belonging place.

traveling companions: JOB AND JOB'S WIFE

I can't begin to imagine what it would feel like to experience the loss that Job endured. Within the span of minutes, he lost his very livelihood—his oxen, donkeys, sheep, and camels—to raids and fire. He lost his servants who cared for his livestock. Most devastating of all, however, Job lost his sons and daughters when the house they were dining in collapsed on top of them (Job 1:13–19).

Sometime later, sores plagued Job from head to toe. In her own particularly low moment, Job's wife told him to "curse God and die." Job responded to her with a resounding *no* through these words: "Shall we receive good from God, and shall we not receive evil?" (Job 2:9–10). To be clear, Job never credited God with the evil—the loss—he experienced. Rather, he eventually realized it was a trial God allowed Satan to deliver because God knew it would bring about future spiritual gain.

Within the pages of Scripture, Job's wife goes down as a disagreeable woman at best and a villain at worst—St. Augustine refers to her as "the devil's accomplice."[4] And while there is good reason to see her in that light, she spoke from a place of hopelessness, a place of fearing she and her husband had been pushed outside of their home country of the kingdom of faith. From Mrs. Job's perspective, the way things were had messed up the way things were supposed to be, and she wanted Job to deal with it via the quickest route possible. I can see why she was tempted to give in to the hopelessness that shrouded her like a heavy blanket in the desert heat.

You and I may not actually curse God for our loss of belonging—although I can't say for certain what I'd do if my children and my livelihood were gone in one fell swoop. However, we can probably identify with that feeling of hopelessness that was at the root of Mrs. Job's words. And we can be strengthened by Job's hopeful response that God had not abandoned him (Job 42:10–17). Because God didn't abandon Job, and he won't abandon us either.

~Belong Blessing~

When you struggle to find your belonging place, know you don't struggle alone. Even as you question where you're supposed to be and with whom, may you model Job and never stop blessing God's name. Even as you feel anger and frustration from unfavorable circumstances being not what you hoped, may God fill you with his infinite hope and reassure you that because of Christ, you are still very much in his favor. May where you want to belong, dear one, and where God calls you to belong be one and the same.

two

Traveling Extremes

We are kingdom receivers, not kingdom builders.

Randy Thompson

WHEN SOMEONE HAS A HARD TIME dealing with a lack of "fit" within a community, she may be tempted to hurry up the process. Pacing back and forth, she believes she needs to *do* something in order to place herself in front of those with whom she'd like to belong. She may think to herself, *Enough of this waiting around and wondering if I'll ever belong. If it's meant to be, it's up to me!* Then she'll slide behind the wheel of her car, hop onto the main highway of visibility, and see where it takes her. She'll do whatever it takes to get herself noticed, including buying her belonging.

Social media teaches us if we post a well-thought-out photo with a clever paragraph next to it, we can do just that. We can "buy" our worth based on who likes our photo or how many comments we accrue. I'm as guilty as the next person of sitting and waiting for someone to "like me" and therefore convince me I belong.

But as my pastor Vince Hoppe explains, we can't buy deliverance from the tyranny of wanting to fit in.[1] Posting and sharing to *give* to others is one thing, but posting and sharing in order to *get* is a dead-end road we don't need to explore. Even if all the "right" people like and comment, it will only give us a counterfeit sense of belonging that lasts but a breath.

Of course, it's possible to be on every social media channel and not take it to this level, to have a healthier perspective that leans toward enjoying the good, creative aspects of it and leans away from using it to fill our need for acceptance. But if we're struggling with our belonging, it's worth honestly evaluating our heart's motive toward what we're expecting to get from the whole online shebang.

Using social media as the fast-track highway to attention looks mighty compelling; it offers limitless opportunities for us to buy into our own selfish motives.[2] If we make fitting in online our chief route to belonging, we'll soon discover we're traveling away from that destination, not closer. We're more susceptible to getting pulled by the collar into a ring of comparison. The more we compare ourselves to others, the more incompetent we feel and the further away we find ourselves from a real sense of belonging. We want to invest our energy connecting with others, not comparing ourselves to others.

Whatever our heart worships or desires more than God will inevitably distance us from him—our true place of belonging. He wants us to taste and see his goodness around us right now. He wants us to belong as his beloved, first with himself and second with our people.

All those online conversations we listen to or participate in do come at a cost. Teens who visit social networking sites more than they see their friends often feel lonely, left out of things, and wish they had more good friends in their life.[3] Another study showed the same to be true for Millennials.[4] I don't fall in either of those age groups, but I know the same has been true for me.

Since the age of ten, I've wanted to be a writer, as well as a mama and coanchor of the *Today Show*. (Jane Pauley, Katie Couric, Savannah, and Hoda—I love you forever!) As a young girl, I filled many a journal writing long, dramatic stories and sentimental poetry. Then came college, marriage, military life, and babies, and I put my love of writing on a shelf for a couple of decades. I picked it back up when my husband deployed, and with it I dusted off the dream of writing a book.

After writing regularly on a blog for a few years and submitting articles to websites and magazines, I complained to friends, "Nobody reads me anyway, so why am I even bothering?" Years passed by, one right after the other, and all I held in my hands was a lot of discouragement because nothing happened fast enough. Instead of relaxing into God's role for me, which asked me to taste and see his goodness each day, my big self wanted to barrel down the road with my own agenda that said, *I'm the one who's good, so pay attention to me!* My own selfish pride positioned me in a "stuck" place of no belonging.

However, pride isn't the only thief that robs us of belonging. Fear snatches it too. Whereas pride tells us we *should* belong where we want to belong, fear tells us we don't *get* to belong where we want to belong. Pride says, *You deserve to belong more than anyone else.* Fear says, *You don't deserve to belong at all.*

A few years ago, that fear of not belonging hit me especially hard on a beach weekend in Hilton Head. I can't tell you how highly I'd anticipated this weekend gathering of fellow writers from an online community I had only recently been invited to join. Generally, I'm comfortable around other people, even people I don't know. I eagerly begin conversations and listen to their stories (thank you for that skill set, United States Air Force). But sometimes, I don't trust that my own stories hold the same interest. So, in that glorious beach house with windows from ceiling to floor, I felt like every writing insecurity of mine had jumped straight through my computer screen and stood in full view for all to see. If that writing community had been composed of US Olympic gymnasts, I felt like the girl in tumbling class turning out cartwheels to their double-twisting-double-layouts.

Now let me be clear: nobody inside the beach house made me feel this way. *Ever.* But I didn't need anyone else to suggest I wasn't up to par. I was my own worst critic, off and running with the enemy's dreadful lies.

On this occasion, when I found myself in a room full of women who weren't just good but excellent at what they do, I was overwhelmed by my own smallness. I started cry-sobbing and resolved then and there to stay within the seafoam and white bathroom for the remainder of the trip. (Yeah, I guess I have a thing for hiding in bathrooms.)

Since I roomed with three other women who would eventually need the bathroom, that wasn't possible. And since I'm not a dainty, quiet crier, they soon discovered me.

I heard a quiet knock on the bathroom door and a gentle, "Kristen? Are you okay?"

I slowly opened the door and saw kind faces wrapped in concern. I smiled weakly and somehow the words just tumbled out.

"I don't belong here. I'm just not good enough!"

These dear women wrapped their arms around me as well as their words and prayers that gave me fresh perspective of who I am in Christ. But I'm not going to lie: I still fight to keep my confidence.

I still fight to remember that belonging is not a state of my circumstances but a state of my soul.

• • •

Feeling too small to belong isn't a bad thing in and of itself. But when our minds travel from Small Street to the corner of Unworthy and Untalented, we've arrived in a dangerous part of town. We're small because of our great God, not because of great people. People are all the same in that we all need Jesus to bridge the miles between us and God.

When it comes to a desire to belong, fear and pride tell us we can do one of two things, at opposite ends of the spectrum. Either we can jump up and down and wave our arms to get noticed (literally or figuratively), or we can give up trying altogether and resolve to hide in the bathroom or our homes or anywhere else void of people. Either way, extremes are the only way to go.

Regularly roving the crowded superhighway of connection leaves me unfulfilled and exhausted. At the same time, remaining locked up inside the protective walls of my home (or bathroom) leaves me lonely and isolated, always an unhealthy place to be. And I'm tired of traveling both these well-worn roads that only take me further away from a place of rest and real belonging.

So, what is the alternative to these options?

We can take a back road way to belonging where we are seen less but sense our belonging more. Where we don't let pride push us into a look-at-me spotlight or let fear shut us up in the dark. Where we give social media its time but give the people around us more. Where we explore the vast "middle area" options, for there are as many back roads as people to travel them.

Maneuvering those well-traversed highways of visibility or slamming the door to the world are traveling extremes. When I begin to feel that lonely ache in my heart and soul because of too little real connection, that's my cue to abandon the loud boulevard for the byways that encourage me to relax into the role God has for me today with those he's placed around me today.

If an event comes across our radar while an invitation to it remains missing, we can refuse to grasp for desperate answers, elbow our way into a prime location, or sink into "I'm a big dumb loser" despair. Instead, we can travel the back road way of looking toward that fertile middle ground of creative possibilities why we are "out" on a particular event. Perhaps attending that event means we're going to miss something more meaningful in the long run. Perhaps our name is on an invitation to another event in the future.

Or God may want our attention on something better suited for us during our present season.

Those words alighted on my heart more than once recently, and finally they prompted me to do a tiny but bold thing to help me quit the traveling extremes: take Facebook off my phone. After debating it for several days, I finally told myself, *Let's do it*. I suppose this felt like an invitation to miss out on Very Important Things.

But delete it I did, and while it's only been a few months since doing so, I already feel lighter, freer, more myself. I still need—and want—some presence on Facebook because of work and because I enjoy seeing life updates from out-of-town family and friends, but I now check it via my laptop. Without it on my phone, I avoid the temptation to plug into it too often. I miss more of the updates from all those secondary folks who don't really need to speak into my life—the receptionist at my eye doctor's office or the friend of a friend I met one time at her Pampered Chef party ten years ago. Therefore, it's not the slow-sieve drain on my sense of belonging. I don't regret it one iota because *not* having it doesn't feel like I'm missing out at all. Instead, it feels like I found a back road toward belonging that points me in the direction of rest and relaxation where God has me today.

While this is something that worked for me, that doesn't mean it's something that will work for you. The Holy Spirit speaks to each of us in unique ways, and he will ask one person to move in a way he doesn't ask another. My back road to belonging will likely look different from yours. But as I wander, I want to use my energies to best serve my priority belonging place. In a culture of disconnection, I want to take the back road way that sets me up to connect with those who matter most.

If you sense God asking you to make a small change in your daily habits, it may be because he wants to point you in a direction closer to your own genuine belonging place, the place that best helps you remain in Christ and relax in God's plan for you this moment, this day.

Let him guide you on that back road, and wander it with windows rolled down and breeze blowing wild.

As you travel along, prepare to receive rather than react.

And prepare to be wowed along the way.

traveling companions:
THE ISRAELITES

When we're on the outside looking in, it takes courage to resist going down the familiar roads we've traveled before. This is something the Israelites knew more than a little about.

In Exodus 14 we read that Pharaoh has just freed the Israelites from captivity, thanks to disastrous plagues sent from the Lord and called forth by Moses. Once freed, Moses and his people are led onward by the Lord, away from Egypt. But sometime shortly thereafter, Pharaoh changed his mind and went after the Israelites. Upon seeing the might and power of Pharaoh's entire army barreling down on them as they camped near the Red Sea, the Israelites panicked and regretted their decision to follow Moses.

As Pharaoh's army drew nearer and nearer, the Israelites were full of fear and began questioning every move that brought them there. Namely, "Is not this what we said to you in Egypt: 'Leave us alone that we may serve the Egyptians'? For it would have been better for us to serve the Egyptians than to die in the wilderness" (Exod. 14:12).

Moses responded, "Fear not, stand firm. . . . The LORD will fight for you" (vv. 13–14).

Then the Lord unzipped the Red Sea's waters so the Israelites could cross. Once they reached the other side unharmed, he brought the waters back together again over the entire Egyptian army.

The Israelites were scared, yes, but they leaned into this promise: *the Lord will fight for you.* And they moved forward.

The Lord who made a way for the sea to swallow an army is the same Lord who will make a way for us to find our own belonging place. We must bravely take that first step forward as we hold the hand of trust. We must believe God has a special road just for you and me, where we won't get lost and where we'll find our place of belonging. "There will be a highway called the Holy Road.... It's for GOD's people exclusively—impossible to get lost on this road. Not even fools can get lost on it" (Isa. 35:8 Message).

Like the Israelites, we can be tempted to do a U-turn back to familiar territory rather than risk an opportunity to find freedom in moving forward. But as Exodus 14 unfolds, we see God had a back road of epic proportions for the Israelites: a Red Sea road toward freedom and real belonging. To get there, however, they had to first walk forward.

As you and I wander the back roads by remaining in Christ and relaxing into his role for us, we're able to stop giving in to pride or panic. We're able to slow down and breathe and, like the Israelites, move forward. We don't need to rush ahead, demanding to be seen. We don't need to withdraw behind walls and doors, believing it's the best option. We can take the third way: the purposeful back road way that asks us to simply focus on God's plan for us today.

~Belong Blessing~

May you know Jesus goes with you as you step out in courage to find your own back road to belonging. Like the Israelites, you do not travel alone. God picked your road for you, and he will lead you to it. May your heart be strengthened as you wait for your place and people to be revealed. May God speak to your heart and soul as to what action you must take to find it. May you use social media as a place to give first rather than get. While you consider what to lean toward as you lean away from the superhighways of connection and isolation, may God bless and keep you as you remember that being seen less is sensing your belonging more.

three

Getting You

The Lord guides us along every step of our journey. His timing
is perfect. He doesn't waste a bit of our wandering.

Sophie Hudson, *Home Is Where My People Are*

WHILE ADDRESSING THE CROWD during a live event, Beth
Moore asked each participant to think on this question: Considering
the various spheres of each person's life, who could own up to feeling
like a misfit on a regular basis? She hoped for enough hands to get
her point across. Instead, she got "a majority thunderous enough to
make the ones who had no such struggle to suddenly feel like—you
guessed it—misfits. The irony in our unshakable sense of alienation
is that many of us are keeping the exact same secret."[1]

For many (most?) of us gals, middle-school trouble sidles up to us
like the person in line behind us at Target with little awareness of personal space. It whispers in our ears, *There's a good reason you struggle
to belong*. There's something about us that's gangly or pudgy, and that
something has nothing to do with our appearance. It might look like

dominating conversations or shrinking from conversations. Being too much or not enough, or both, depending on the circumstances.

Maybe you fret you lost approval because of your school choice for your kids or who you voted for. Whatever it is, it's your other-brand of awkward, and it stands sentry at the door telling you, *Nice try, but forget it. You don't fit in here.* In a social sense, you see yourself as a nicer version of one of Cinderella's stepsisters, who can't get her big ugly foot into that petite glass slipper.

When my daughter was in middle school, she came home one day with a tale as old as time, and it goes like this: at the beginning of middle school, she and two other girls were thick as thieves. They spent hours upon hours together doing all the typical things middle schoolers do. Later on, however, she began to hear how they were getting together without her. She didn't think anything about it for a long while. After all, the other two girls lived close to one another, so it was easy for them to hang out. Then things became more overt. The other two girls would make plans to shop together while sitting next to my daughter at the lunch table, dress in twinning style, or ping-pong sleepover dates between their two houses. My girl sat right there as, time after time, they talked about hanging out in front of her but never with her. One afternoon, as I picked my girl up after school, she hopped into the car, shut the door hard, and sighed. She said matter-of-factly, "Well, Mama, I need to face facts. I've been 'othered.'"

It seemed the trio had turned into a duo-plus-one.

This brought to mind times when I've been "othered," as well as times I've "othered" somebody else. Those memories make me wince like I do when someone tells me bad news. *Lord, forgive me for those times I've knowingly or inadvertently pushed someone outside her belonging place.*

• • •

While getting "othered" in the way my daughter experienced changes our place and people to a certain degree, it also shows how life wanders this way and that, how our belonging place in one season isn't always the same place in another. Sometimes a relational road stops at a dead-end tangle of brush and fallen trees.

A lot of wandering masquerades as setbacks, dead ends, and broken roads. This wandering is necessary but sometimes frustrating or even annoying. We're always be-coming, and that doesn't always come by direct route.

Author Shelly Miller writes this of wandering:

> Uncertainty reminds us that the mystery is where God resides. His ways are rarely straightforward. Wandering is required work because we need to know we are loved first. And coming to belief about God's love isn't always a straight line.[2]

Yes, uncertainty swirls all around us when we're on the outside looking in. We want to know why we can't belong where we want to belong, and when that's going to change. But if we embrace the wandering component on our back road, we embrace the mystery— where God resides. Some things we must wait to know, and it's okay to wander as we wonder and wait.

Jesus certainly gets how this journey includes a fair bit of wandering as we move from where we are to where we'd like to be. As Jesus traveled from town to town, he periodically took out-of-the-way roads that added miles to his journey.[3] He experienced delays of his own. A notable one occurs in Luke 11, when some of Jesus's dearest loved ones, Mary and Martha, sent him word that their brother Lazarus was ill. They probably thought, in doing so, that Jesus would leave lickety-split and make his way to them in Bethany. However, that's not what happened. "So, when he heard that Lazarus was ill, he stayed two days longer in the place where he was. Then after this he said to the disciples, 'Let us go to Judea again'" (John 11:6–7). *The Message* paraphrase adds character to this whole picture:

> Jesus loved Martha and her sister and Lazarus, but oddly, when he heard that Lazarus was sick, he stayed on where he was for two more days. (vv. 5–6)

Yeah, sometimes God works in mysterious ways. But sometimes he also works in just plain *odd* ways.

More than that, the disciples thought it was foolish to head to Bethany in the first place, because it was only a couple miles from Jerusalem, where the Jews wanted to stone Jesus. After Jesus gave his disciples their travel itinerary, the disciples responded in John 11:8 with something akin to, "Why in the Sam Hill are we going back to where people wanted to kill you?"

When Jesus and his disciples finally arrived in Bethany, Lazarus had been dead and in the tomb for four days. Even knowing the miracles Jesus was capable of performing, some of the disciples must have wondered what purpose lay in going so late. Martha wondered too, and she wasted no time in giving her opinion. "Lord, if you had been here, my brother would not have died" (v. 21). A few verses later, Mary told him the exact same thing. Under a veil of exasperation, they echoed what Scripture tells us others believed as well: *If you'd shaken a leg and gotten here sooner, Lazarus would be alive.*

I would've said the same thing, probably in the most accusatory voice in my arsenal. Considering your own life circumstances, maybe you've asked something similar.

Lord, if you'd acted sooner on this management problem, I wouldn't have lost my job.

If you'd intervened earlier in that unacceptable relationship, I wouldn't have lost my spouse.

If you'd prevented my body from getting the cancer cells, I wouldn't have this health crisis hanging over my head.

If you'd been more aware of my circumstances, I wouldn't be without a belonging place right now.

Jesus understands our frustration, and he can't help but move in a way that maximizes the consequences for good. Because of Jesus's delay in getting to Bethany, many people who witnessed the event came to believe in him. Their faith was strengthened, and God received all the credit. That is why he delayed before raising Lazarus from the dead, and that's why he delays in our own lives. Jesus always moves as the Father directs. Not always as we might wish but always for our benefit. Jesus's wandering—and ours—is never purposeless.

Like us, Jesus also experienced frustration within the delays. In Matthew 17, a man approaches him to beg healing help for his son. When his disciples could not drive out the demon causing the boy's seizures, Jesus's annoyance showed up in highlighter yellow, although not because they couldn't perform the miracle. Frustrated that some in attendance were still obstinate toward God, he said with undoubted exasperation:

> "What a generation! No sense of God! No focus to your lives! How many times do I have to go over these things? How much longer do I have to put up with this? Bring the boy here." He ordered the afflicting demon out—and it was out, gone. From that moment on the boy was well. (Matt. 17:17–18 Message)

Jesus knew how this singular event—as well as his delay in raising Lazarus from the dead—played into the big picture of God's plan for him. But that doesn't mean he didn't get frustrated with the people and circumstances along the way. He likely had moments he wanted to yank someone by the collar and tell them, "Get with the program already!"

• • •

Yeah, the way God moves or the places he asks us to travel may confuse us more than comfort us in the moment. The timing may be terrible. But because Jesus's wandering had purpose, our wandering has purpose. It's not aimless. It's an opportunity to trust in what we can't see but know because of his dependable character.

Within our wandering, we know God doesn't mind us sharing our honest struggles and frustrations with him. The psalms are full of honest laments to the Lord, and he doesn't expect us to pretend like we're all-fired excited about the "spiritual formation" our struggles offer while telling our sadness and disappointment to take a seat. The important thing is that, along with lamenting, we still land on the hope that God only allows pain in our life if it will give us future gain.

And as my friend Alli discovered, God will sometimes allow confusion in your life for the purpose of refining your journey.

As Alli and her husband excitedly prepared to move from Colorado to California—where Alli was born and raised—she rested in the security that comes with knowing beyond a shadow of a doubt that she and her family moved in the Lord's direction for them. In multiple ways, God led her and her husband to know they were to live in the foothills of the Sierras. With the timing right, they excitedly looked for a house in that area.

However, out of the clear blue their circumstances changed. The sale of the house they were set to close on fell through because of an odd technicality. Inexplicably, the same thing happened a second time. In Alli's mind, the Lord shut the door tightly on their move not once but twice, and she wondered if she'd really heard God's voice in the first place. Should she and her family not move to California after all?

Then God brought Alli to the passage of Acts 16 where he led Paul, Silas, and Timothy to preach the Word within a particular region. As they traveled, however, doors closed left and right.

> They went to Phrygia, and then on through the region of Galatia. Their plan was to turn west into Asia province, but the Holy Spirit blocked that route. So they went to Mysia and tried to go north to Bithynia, but the Spirit of Jesus wouldn't let them go there either. (Acts 16:6–8 Message)

Twice Paul and the others tried to enter territory within the Lord's direction, and twice they were hindered. However, Paul didn't give up. Even as God shut tight the door on their original destinations, he brought Paul a vision that clarified his plan for the missionaries.

> That night Paul had a dream: A Macedonian stood on the far shore and called across the sea, "Come over to Macedonia and help us!"

The dream gave Paul his map. We went to work at once getting things ready to cross over to Macedonia. All the pieces had come together. We knew now for sure that God had called us to preach the good news to the Europeans. (vv. 9–10 Message)

These passages confirmed for Alli that, like Paul, she had indeed heard God correctly all along. Paul was convinced of his mission and knew what he had to do. He was always on the right path; it just needed refining. Alli and her family were on the right path too. They just had to do a bit of wandering as God refined their destination. The pieces came together when he eventually led them to the specific town and belonging place they would call home—in the Sierra foothills.[4]

Back road routes are often wandered as we journey toward the place God has for us. We shouldn't always assume a closed door means we're not hearing the Lord correctly. Sometimes a door shut is only a direction changed or a path refined.

• • •

Fellow back road wanderer, Jesus identifies with us and knows what it's like to be on the outside looking in, to be displaced and driven out. He was outside looking in on several occasions, not the least of which was when he was crucified *outside* the city gates (Heb. 13:12). In spite of this, he still participated in life when and where his Father asked him to. He invites us to not only live this way but believe that doing so will bring us a sense of belonging too.

As we sit in the comforting knowledge that Jesus gets what it's like to be us, it's important to remember that no one on this earth will ever get us in the same way. No flesh and blood person could ever be the never-disappointing person Jesus is. I'll admit first that sometimes I'd love nothing more than to fit perfectly well with the people in my life, like the smooth pieces of a puzzle all put together. If your frustration over a lack of belonging comes from wanting to jam your own puzzle pieces into place, find real relief in the fact that they're not supposed to fit that way. Beth Moore beautifully puts it this way:

> We search for the ultimate church that meets all our preferences in worship, Word, and companionship, and lo and behold, sometimes we think we've discovered it. Then, just about the time we settle in, disappointment inevitably comes in one area or another and dashes our high hopes into the nearest ditch. We then have a choice: forsake that assembly in search of another, or stick around to see what kind of mosaic Jesus could build with a cooperative bunch of misfit pieces.[5]

Whether in our church, our family, our neighborhood, our school, our job, our town, or our region of the country or world, we will always carry with us enough rough edges and pokey corners to never completely fit. We need the love and help of Christ to solidify the space between us and someone else, until all our broken, rough, and jagged parts make one distinct, brazen, and wholly beautiful mosaic.

Yes, sometimes we're called to leave a place. However, if we find perennial dissatisfaction with every circle we're in, odds are good we're not called to abandon every one altogether. Until we leave room for Christ to enter the in-between places, you and I will have a hard time being content where God has placed us.

There's no perfect place for you to belong, but Jesus does perfectly understand all your struggles and frustrations to find your own, imperfect-but-just-right-for-you belonging place. Settle into the back road journey that wanders the winding way and gives you ample time to sit with Jesus on the outside. Take it one mile at a time, showing up where he wants you to show up moment by moment.

I talk about this with my girl when she again mentions sitting outside that friend group. "Right now, my love, you're being asked to take the wandering road home to friendship. But take heart: Jesus gets how hard this is, how frustrating all the slow moving is. Jesus gets you . . . and God will get you where you're supposed to be. Just don't stop being the amazing girl you are. Keep participating in your own life, even if others aren't inviting you to participate in theirs the way you'd like."

May each of us enduring a similar struggle remember to keep participating in our own life. To keep showing up where we're asked to show up, instead of where we wish we could. To share with God our honest struggles and feelings. To fling love extravagantly over every inch of our circles of influence. To trust that Jesus, the one who traveled back roads so others would know they belonged, will always meet us on our own back road as well.

Jesus gets it . . . and he's got you.

traveling companion:
HOLLEY

Holley stared in wonder at two pink lines on a pregnancy test—a dream fulfilled for her and her husband, Mark, after two years of trying to start a family. Then those two pink lines changed to heart-breaking red.[6] Holiday after holiday passed without Holley becoming pregnant again, and she mourned the happy ending that eluded this part of her hopes and desires.

For almost a decade, Holley wanted to be a mama in the way the world told her she should, in the way that seemed so easy for other women. During that time, Holley and Mark went through years of grief, loss, doctors' appointments, and serious wrestling with God. Then, in his subtle, gentle way, God began showing Holley there was more than one way to become a mother. One Mother's Day, God pointed her to Genesis 3:20, where Eve is named "the mother of all living." From that moment on, Holley knew that all women bring life to this world. For her, however, that new life wouldn't happen through a physical baby.[7]

Given our culture's intense focus on family, this was no easy thing for Holley to accept.

At first, speaking this part of her story out loud seemed at best outrageous and at worst possibly un-christian. She faced a lot of well-meaning but hard questions from others. Holley knew that what others believed she and Mark should do to build a family was not what God called them to do.

Then Holley watched a documentary about foster kids aging out of the system at eighteen. Learning this stirred something deep inside her, and as she watched the screen she kept saying out loud, "That's not okay, that's not okay." When people asked Holley if she and her husband thought about adoption, she began to answer, "If we ever adopt, our kid will be a twenty-year-old."[8]

A few years later, as Holley regularly brought new life into this world through her many heart-healing books, she was invited to a banquet at Saving Grace, a local transitional living home for girls aging out of the foster system, girls who would otherwise be homeless.[9] While at that banquet, Holley met a girl named Lovelle, a twenty-year-old resident of Saving Grace. Holley and Mark began spending more and more time with Lovelle. They showed up at the finish line of her half marathon. They invited her into their home and into their everyday, ordinary life, and in due course Lovelle legally changed her name and wholeheartedly became their daughter.

Holley and Mark's path to becoming parents was anything but a straight line. It was a wandering, meandering path where closed doors were not endings but direction changes. Holley became a mama not in the way the world told her she should but in the way the Lord destined her to. She and Mark built a family as the Lord intended, in a less traditional but just as meaningful way. And once Lovelle entered their lives, they discovered God's idea of what their family would look like fit them beautifully.

At one time, Holley put all her mothering hope in two pink lines on a pregnancy test. She put her hope in that part of herself looking like she thought it should. In the end, however, Holley put her hope in belonging where God intended her to: within the beautiful lines of a family love story she never expected.[10]

~Belong Blessing~

When you believe you're in a season of wandering around a barren belonging landscape, may you know you don't wander purposelessly. God is aware of every bump and bend, and Jesus walks with you through every setback and delay. May you never stop participating in your own life, even through the mystery—because God is moving *for* you in your life. May you remember Jesus was brought outside so you could be brought inside forever. The Lord truly gets you—what you like and don't like, all the curious and conventional things you bring to the table. May you know he will guide you gently but firmly to the place you belong.

four

Extending Kindness
to Yourself

You can't expect to be perfect
It's a fight you've gotta forfeit
You belong to me whatever you do
So lay down your weapon, darling
Take a deep breath and believe that I love you.

Andrew Peterson, "Be Kind to Yourself"

ONE SPRING EVENING during my junior year of high school, I remember walking from the living room of my home down the hallway toward my bedroom. As I did so, my daddy's voice tiptoed from my parents' bedroom at the other end of the hallway to my ears. Given the silent pause after he talked, I figured he was on the phone. I kept walking toward my bedroom, not giving any thought to his conversation—until he said my name. That made me stop and do what most teens like to do: eavesdrop to see what secret information I could uncover.

From what I gathered, the person Daddy talked to was asking how I was doing in school, specifically if he or my mom had to get on to me to do homework or study for tests. Twenty-five years later, I still hear Daddy saying, "Get on to Kristen? Naw, we don't have to get on to her about schoolwork. And even if we did, we could never be as hard on Kristen as she is on herself."

Boy howdy, that was the truth then, and in some ways it's still the truth now. I've spent many a day emotionally black and blue from being too hard on myself. I often replay conversations in my head and berate myself because I said one thing instead of another. I'm not even talking about rude things, although I've certainly had to ask forgiveness more than once for talking ugly. Rather, I find myself backing up and thinking of choice words or phrases I should've said that might've conveyed my idea better. I've spent more than a little time asking my husband's opinion on something I said to someone else, wanting his assurance my words or actions didn't come across poorly.

"Should I have said this?"

"Do you think that came off as offensive?"

"Would it have been better to do that?"

(You can imagine what a "barn-burner" this is for him!) And for every question I ask out loud, I ask three more in my head. Of course, a healthy amount of self-awareness and care for the feelings of others are important things to keep in mind. However, if we find the scales tipping toward giving a disproportionate amount of time and head space to these kinds of thoughts and questions, then we need to also be self-aware enough to look at why we're doing it. Because constantly second-guessing ourselves isn't kind behavior toward ourselves.

Not only that, it also serves the lie that says, *Wherever I am, I don't belong there. Sure, I was in with this gal or that group of folks before. But now, that thing I said or did (or didn't say or do) probably changed all of that, so I'm out. I've ruined it all.* It prevents us from relaxing and settling in to where God has us today, certain our mistakes are too big for grace's mantle.

The enemy of our hearts and souls condemns us through all kinds of accusations, and if you're anything like me, you're inclined to listen and absorb every single one of them. What's more, you might add, "Oh yeah? You don't know the half of it. I'm so much worse than even *you* know."

It's an exhausting, graceless, fruitless way to live, constantly at bat against ourselves.

Another way unkindness-to-self shows up? Over-apologizing.

A few years ago, I sat in a booth at a Cheesecake Factory with five girlfriends. As I chatted with my people, I scanned the menu up and down, asking myself what I should get. My rumbly stomach answered that, basically, every offering sounded fantastic. When it came time to place my order, I still hesitated with indecision. Looking up at the waiter, I apologized for taking so long. And then once I did spell out my order, for Chinese chicken salad, I quickly changed my mind and said, "Oh wait! I'm so sorry, but I'll have the fish tacos after all!" I proceeded to apologize again for being so difficult.

The waiter tapped his pencil on his pad, eyed the group collectively, and said, "Does she always apologize this much?"

As if they had rehearsed it, my friends responded in a singular chorus, "Yeeees."

Guess what I did next? Yeah, I apologized again for apologizing.

Gah, sometimes I get on my own nerves something fierce.

This act of over-apologizing is particularly sneaky because it appears in a gray wool coat that looks a lot like humility, not unkindness. However, once that coat is removed, the bright neon clothing underneath screams self-sabotaging unkindness to oneself. It's a simple thing, really. But it is through such everyday, simple behaviors as my apologizing in the restaurant that we reflect the deeper belief that our existence needs toning down.

Being endlessly hard on myself. Questioning what I say or do. Apologizing for simple things like changing my mind about something. I have a few theories that explain this part of my personality, but they all seem to fall under one lie in my mind that I've twirled into truth: *In one way or another, I don't have a right to belong in this world as myself.*

Maybe, like me, you're guilty of struggling to belong because you're fearful you don't measure up in any number of ways, including having what it takes to complete a certain job or be a valuable friend. But underneath, you're really concerned you don't measure up for God. You live as though he's surely disappointed in you, annoyed with you, or hostile toward you. Deep down in your heart, you worry your sense of *not* belonging is punishment for your not-enoughness. So you step on the never-ending treadmill of "trying and striving" in order to please him.

In reality, you don't need to try to please God, because through his Son Jesus, he's already pleased with you.

After taking in the emerging blossoms of the bougainvillea planted around her property, Leeana Tankersley wrote these words about the chronic habit of over-apologizing:

> I'm more and more convinced that God is pretty much always trying to tell us, "Yeah, I got it. You're not perfect. But do you know you're beautiful?" You are brittle twigs and you are flowering vines and you are dormant beauty and you are flashing fuchsia. And it's all beautiful. Let. Yourself. Emerge.
>
> It's OK to let us see you. It's OK to bloom, blossom, vine. It's OK. You don't have to shrink for fear of actually being seen. You don't have to whisper for fear of actually being heard. You don't have to apologize for yourself anymore. You are allowed to take up space in your life and in this world.[1]

Leeana's words point me to the only message that heals this perfectionist-leaning heart: Christ, the only flawless human being, died so my flawed self could absolutely belong in this world.

And because of his saving work, God makes a way for me and every other person to belong where he or she is supposed to belong, without apology.

As a high schooler, I stood several inches taller than most of my friends, both girls and guys. To combat the "singled out" feeling being tall gave me, I would purposely slouch down in an attempt to blend in with my shorter posse. Shorter meant less noticeable, more belonging. Slouching was the way I apologized for my height.

Now, as a woman over five foot ten, I love my height. If I could go back to that high schooler and tell her to just ride that vertical tide of God-given height, I would. I'd tell her it'll all be worth it one day, that she'll relish every inch. I'd tell her that until that day arrives, please remember God made her this way; he calls her wondrously beautiful, and for all that is good and holy, please quit slouching and shrinking and hiding already.

I'd tell her she is a part of God's creation, and his creation never, ever requires apology.

I can't tell my high school self any of these things, but I can tell it to my grown-up self. I can tell her to sit down in her favorite corner of the sofa, to grab her softest blanket and tuck it around her curled-up feet. Like Jesus told the waves and wind to *Shhhhh*, I can tell that legalistic, ungracious part of myself to *Hush on down*. I can tell her she has all the right in this world to take up space in her life. I can tell her Jesus loves her, and she can begin living right this second out of how the Creator made her and out of Jesus's love for her.

You can do the same for your own grown-up girl too.

Instead of viewing ourselves through the lens of apology, what if we viewed ourselves through the lens of Jesus instead? What if we took off our wonky, smudgy glasses and stopped living life with a posture of *I'm sorry*? We're allowed to have our own thoughts, feelings, and opinions. If we trip over words, don't say what we should, or do something we shouldn't, it's *okay*. We can allow grace to do its good work. *I'm sorry* should be saved for situations that warrant repentance. It should be used in circumstances where we need forgiveness. It shouldn't be used because we believe we're intrinsically sorry or no good.

We're not dingbats or deadweight.

• • •

You have the right to exist in this world. You have the right to be a real part of God's plan for you in your family and community. You can enthusiastically show up for your assignment instead of apologetically shrinking from it. You can courageously own the present and future gifts you hold from God *with you* and Christ *in you*. Let that lead you to intentionally listen to God's affirmation rather than the enemy's accusations.

Let that lead you back to the gospel, again and again and again.

I know as much as anyone how hard it is to kick insecurity out the back door. But when we commit to tackling it on a case-by-case basis, we are able to take each individual issue to Jesus and trade our insecurity for the security found in God's favor. We're able to practice self-compassion and kindness by refusing to treat ourselves like our own enemy.

We can be an advocate for ourselves as we talk about ourselves with a different vocabulary, believing we're worth the effort.

So go ahead and change your mind about that order. Don't worry about taking the time to put your wallet back in your purse before you leave the checkout aisle. Believe that if you relaxed and didn't carefully choose all your words, your people would still love you.

Just wave away that lie that whispers *you're too much* when you laugh too loud, talk too long, or cry too often. Just turn your back on that feeling that shouts *you're not enough* when you listen long, share little, or stay where you are.

Let yourself be loved in your most tender places by the One who knows you best and loves you best. Be kind to yourself by refusing to apologize for yourself, by being the singularly treasured gift you are to this world.

And let yourself confidently walk forward with a deeper sense of belonging as you relax and settle in to where God has you today.

The other day, I read afresh Colossians 2:10:

And in Christ you have been brought to fullness. He is the head over every power and authority. (NIV)

We have been given *fullness* in Christ. Today, we are already complete. We are worthy enough and talented enough and just plain *enough*. I repeat this to myself over and over, and before long, the devil static fades past the horizon. It is then I find confidence to take the road less traveled to where God has me today.

If God is for me, who can be against me?

May it not be me.

traveling companion:
MARY, MOTHER OF JESUS

I love that Scripture is full of questions, questions asked by God and regular people like us. Clearly, God doesn't mind us throwing some vertical inquiries in his direction. Sometimes we don't suffer from unbelief as much as we just want a safe place and honest means by which to grasp a better understanding. This was the case with Mary's questions found in Luke 2.

Luke 1:26–38 unfolds with the angel Gabriel quite literally dropping in on Mary to give her a message like no other woman had ever received. That message was the starting pistol fired before a cross-country journey toward the destination of Jesus's birth.

As Scripture unfolds, we learn the angel Gabriel told the stunned young woman,

> Do not be afraid, Mary, for you have found favor with God. And behold, you will conceive in your womb and bear a son, and you shall call his name Jesus. He will be great and will be called the Son of the Most High. And the Lord God will give to him the throne of his father David, and he will reign over the house of Jacob forever, and of his kingdom there will be no end. (Luke 1:30–33)

In verse 34, we read Mary's response: "How will this be, since I am a virgin?" In other words, "As a virgin with a fiancé, how could I possibly travel this road?"

Even as she believed it would happen—she believed what the Lord spoke through the angel would be accomplished—she struggled to believe *how* it would happen. She was an engaged woman who'd never been with a man. How could she belong within this story?

Gabriel wasted no time in explaining she would become pregnant through the Holy Spirit, and Mary's most pressing question was answered. She belonged within this story because the Lord chose her, and his presence went with her.

However, I also wonder if Mary's original "How will this be?" hid other queries beyond the logistical one. Did she believe she was enough to fulfill this mission? Did she believe she had what it takes to mother such greatness? Parenting any kid has its daunting moments. Surely parenting the "Son of the Most High" whose kingdom would last forever would seem overwhelming if not impossible. It's not a stretch to believe Mary might've considered another unspoken thought: *Am I good enough to do what God's asking me to do?*

The angel's response is the response for all those worried that belonging is an impossibility: "For nothing will be impossible with God" (v. 37).

Mary didn't argue or tell him all the reasons she wasn't the right woman for the job. She didn't apologize for her house being a mess or for asking a question. She simply answered, "Let it be to me according to your word" (v. 38).

She listened to the Lord's affirmation rather than the enemy's accusations. She took God at his word and enthusiastically showed up for her assignment.

Like Mary, our *enoughness* is not a factor in where God places us. It's inconsequential. God chose you to be where you are, and he will make a way for you to belong.

~Belong Blessing~

May the Lord quiet your soul as he speaks to your heart, *You are just right, just as you are.* May you lose all temptation to apologize for taking up space in this beautiful world and instead celebrate God choosing you. May you be less hard on yourself as you believe God is truly pleased with you because of Jesus's saving work for you. May any lingering questions be used as pavement that keeps you walking toward God rather than away. And may you delight in the place God has for you, knowing he offers his best for you.

five

Singing Loudly

How it must break his heart when we walk around so desperate
for a love He waits to give us each and every day.

Lysa TerKeurst, *Uninvited*

ONCE WE BECOME MORE AWARE of our need to be kind to
ourselves and start acting on that need, the dust begins to settle a little
in front of us, and we can see God's back road way for us with more
clarity. That back road is God's gift to us, a tailor-made place empty
of expectations and full of possibilities. We can begin to look at belonging where we're supposed to belong as the unique people we are.

However, if you're still learning this because your longtime default
is to be unkind to yourself and apologize for existing, seeing that road
through the kicked-up dust is harder to do. It requires a monumental
shift in thinking. You're likely used to presenting yourself as you think
you *should* be—or how others try to talk you into being—rather than
as you really are.

Not long ago, I chaperoned a field trip for my daughter's choir to an
amusement park in Denver. While there are plenty of school-related

kid things I'm not going to jump up and down to volunteer for (*cough cough* PTO *cough*), I'm a weirdo mom who likes going on field trips with the kids. Give me all the chatty girls. Give me all the bantering boys. Give me my perked-up ears listening to what's going on around the middle school without acting like I'm actually listening. I guess it's the former school teacher in me that just digs those kiddos, even if I don't enjoy being out of the house by 5:30 a.m., as this trip required.

The first purpose of this particular field trip was to participate in a choir competition. We arrived at the location on a gorgeous, sunshine-drenched morning, the air cool and invigorating. After entering the park, we walked toward the building hosting the competition. The choir teacher ushered the kids to carpeted risers in a corner of the room for warm-ups, and we parents seated ourselves in metal chairs at the opposite side of the room.

When it was our kids' turn to sing, sing they did. In matching tie-dyed tees and various shades of denim, the whole gang sang their music-loving hearts out. I trained my eyes on my girl in the middle row, watching her do her thing. I couldn't pick her voice out in the group, but I could tell by her confident facial expressions she performed to her liking. When she sang a duet at the beginning of "Beauty and the Beast," I could hear her sing the high notes with clarity. She hit her low notes in tune. She performed the dance moves in rhythm as she kept her eyes on the choir teacher throughout. Because she and the group had practiced each song time after time, they did what they needed to do when it counted.

Practice never makes perfect, as perfection is a mirage that disappears before you arrive. But practice with patience makes excellence, and that's always worth the effort, no matter the results.

The competition ended by 9:00 a.m., and that left eight whole hours to explore all the amusement park offered. As it turns out, my daughter didn't need eight hours to explore. She only needed a few hours to investigate all the park had to offer, which was primarily roller coasters.

At one point, after eyeing another roller coaster her friends itched to ride, she turned to me, shoulders shrugging, and said, "I don't know why I can't have as much fun here as my friends."

Having been to other amusement parks with her, including Disney World, I knew Faith didn't like roller coasters. But sometimes a girl needs her mama to remind her of these things.

I looked at her and replied, "Baby, it's because you don't love roller coasters, and that's okay! They don't have to be your thing." She acknowledged this, but when another friend came up asking her to join in on another roller-coaster ride, her confidence waned.

It's easier to sing loudly and confidently with the crowd, but get on stage alone, and it's a lot harder to do. Get asked to do something that really isn't your thing, something you *know* isn't your thing, and you doubt your position. It's one thing to know this about yourself, but it's another to be okay with it—especially when everyone else is more than okay with the opposite. Enthusiastic about the opposite.

And just like that, your sense of belonging within that group flies up, up, and away.

But at times like these, it seems we have a choice. We can dig toward the bottom of why we feel we don't belong and become okay with that part of ourselves, or we can charge ahead as we think we should be rather than how we are.

So my girl and I talked things out. Since she has ridden roller coasters on several occasions, we both knew she couldn't chalk up her distaste for them to fear or being scared to try one. We talked about how she is a highly sensitive person—that is, her nervous system and sensory levels are easily overwhelmed—and amusement parks throw a whole lot of stimuli at you all at once. Like me, she gets overwhelmed by hours of amped up music and constant screaming.

My daughter wanted to love roller coasters so she could have that sense of belonging with her friends. But as we sat in the shade of the trees enjoying our sack lunches of peanut butter and jelly sandwiches, she re-realized that *Nope, roller coasters aren't my thing.*

Over the course of the day, she rode a few rides and thoroughly enjoyed them. But if she didn't want to ride something, she didn't. Instead, she would grab a snack or visit the animals in a nearby exhibit, and by the end of the day, she could still say she had fun doing what she wanted and fun not doing what she didn't.

She had fun because she discovered more about where she belonged *and* because she became more okay with not belonging where she didn't. She could belong with her friends in spite of a few different personality traits and interests.

She had fun because on that hot day in Denver, she learned a bit more about herself. In the learning, she could more confidently sing the song God created her to sing.

Isn't that what we all want? The confidence to step into the outline of our real selves, really assured that God wasn't having an off day or a case of "this'll do" when he dreamed us up? We want to belong as we really are rather than trying to "fit in" with an unauthentic version of ourselves. God only creates originals, and accepting this brings a deeper sense of belonging. Accepting this honors his creative work that is us and is done through us.

However, knowing this and acting like it's true are two different things. Isn't it a bit scary to act like it's true?

I'd like to suggest something: Can we just be a little scared but begin walking down that back road anyway? Just doing the thing—moving on down the road—helps us release some of the fear-wrapped lie that says we can't belong as we truly are.

We don't have to go it alone, either.

And your ears shall hear a word behind you, saying, "This is the way, walk in it," when you turn to the right or when you turn to the left. (Isa. 30:21)

As we walk wobbly kneed on our back road, following God's direction, we can know our back road is where God tells us, *There is freedom along the way, dear one. There is freedom in holding on to the quirks and perks of your personality and in letting go of what isn't a part of your wiring.*

> Among those who belong to Christ, everything connected with getting our own way and mindlessly responding to what everyone else calls necessities is killed off for good—crucified. (Gal. 5:24 Message)

Yes, belonging to Christ means he's first and we're second, so we sacrifice our "right" to get our way and become okay playing second fiddle. Belonging to Christ also means belonging as God's necessary, singular creation. It's owning what he says is necessary—and not necessary—for you to sing your song.

It's not a necessity for my girl to love roller coasters. It's not necessary for me to love elbowy crowds. It's not necessary for my friend Rebecca, who would rather be hog-tied to a fence post than be in a car for twelve hours, to take a cross-country road trip when there are pilots and planes that'll fly her there lickety-split. It's okay for the roller coaster lovers to scream their heads off on every loop-de-loop. It's good and right to know what we like and move from there, but it's also good and right to know what we *don't* like and move from there as well.

Don't berate yourself for not belonging where God never intended for you to belong.

Do find joy in singing *loudly* the song you're created to sing because of the confidence you have in how your Creator designed you. In short: don't be afraid to be you.

Be you and be you well.

As Jesus meanders down your back road with you, let him nudge you toward a confident posture in this. We can be ourselves well when we let the truth of Christ's saving work accomplished on our behalf enter our inner places, behind all the curtains and masks and *I-should-be-like-this* thoughts. None of them are God's idea for you.

Several years ago, Kara Tippetts, author of the book *Mundane Faithfulness*, spoke at my church's women's retreat. One of her comments seared itself to my heart. On this whole notion of being me well, it acts as a compass that steers me in the right direction. She said, "Don't *should* all over yourself." Don't live life by what you think you should do, but by what God calls you to do and how he's wired you. Those are the necessities. The rest, the *shouldities*, can be heaved into the ditch for today—for forever. We bury the *shouldities* and let Christ's desires for us rise up inside us over and over again.

Christ's yoke is laid-back and light, like the song played to the rhythm of his heartbeat for you. Like a song whose tune is original to you.

Sing your song without apology.

Sing it with kindness.

Sing it with intention.

Sing it with praise to your Dad in heaven.

Sing it because it'll do you a world of good and make God grin. Let it be the music you meander to down your back road to belonging.

Danish Christian theologian Søren Kierkegaard said, "Now, by the help of God, I shall become myself."[1] Let God help you become yourself by making you brave enough to be as you are.

Let him help you to relax, to be you and be you well.

With time, patience, and practice, let your song's notes ring out as loudly as you please, be it from the sharp turn of a roller coaster or the cozy corner of a quiet café.

Here's to being you and being you well.

traveling companion: LEAH

Leah knew rejection in profoundly painful ways, not to mention what it's like to be on the outside looking in because of who she was—and wasn't.

While Leah is often portrayed as a homely woman, several Bible translations describe her eyes as tender, even lovely (Gen. 29:17 KJV, TLB). Well, Leah may have had pretty eyes, but Rachel, her younger sister, was head-to-toe gorgeous. Rachel got more than a little attention from others, including a man named Jacob.

As we read through Genesis 29, we learn that Jacob, a relative of Leah and Rachel, came to stay with their family. Upon arrival, he made it clear to Leah and Rachel's father, Laban, that he wanted to marry Rachel. When the time came for him to do so, Laban gave a wedding feast for the bridegroom, who presumed he would be marrying Rachel. However, as the ceremony began, Laban took Leah, not Rachel, and gave her to Jacob (Gen. 29:23). We aren't told of Rachel's whereabouts at this time. We aren't told if Leah willingly went along with this scheme or if she was just doing what she was told—a probable response, as most women in those days didn't get a choice in these matters. Whatever the surrounding circumstances, we know that by the time Jacob and Leah married, it was dark. Leah wore a veil, and Jacob had likely enjoyed more than a little alcohol. He didn't realize he'd married Leah till morning—when he noticed Leah lying next to him instead of Rachel.

When Jacob questioned Laban about the whole affair, Laban offered a made-up, flimsy excuse about it not being custom to marry the younger daughter before the older.[2] Regardless of what disgraceful motive Laban had for switching brides, the marriage was a done deal. Scripture goes on to say that after Jacob's wedding week with Leah, he married Rachel, and "he loved Rachel more than Leah, and served Laban for another seven years" (v. 30).

As time went on, the Lord took notice that Leah was unloved, so he "opened her womb" (v. 31). Leah gave Jacob one son right after another, which culturally would've been a big feather in Jacob's cap. At the very least, this should've made him smile upon Leah. Yet this doesn't seem to be what Jacob did. After giving birth to her third son, Levi, Leah said, "Now this time my husband will be attached to me, because I have borne him three sons" (v. 34).

One commentary explains her situation this way:

> Having been tricked into marrying Leah, Jacob never really loved her
> or her children. Indeed, he does not ever seem to have regarded her
> as his wife. But she was desperate for his affection. . . . Her deepest
> desire was that "*my husband will love me now*" (v. 32).[3]

All she wanted was the one thing that alluded her: her husband's
love and affection. I wonder how often she cried herself to sleep
at night, reliving the day's events that found her ignored and over-
looked. I wonder how often she looked at her young boys and took
notice of something cute or funny they did, only to mourn all over
again that she didn't have a caring husband with whom to share those
things.

I wonder if the loneliness of rejection hollowed out her heart a
little at a time as she wished away the parts of herself that weren't
enough for Jacob. As she wished she could be someone he'd love.

Perhaps a part of her blamed herself. Maybe she thought she deserved Jacob's cold shoulder because when she and Jacob had been
alone on their wedding night, she didn't clue him in that she wasn't
Rachel. We don't know because Scripture doesn't tell us. But what
it does tell us is by the time Leah birthed her fourth son, she had a
shift in her thinking.

After her first three sons, Leah was hopeful that they would bring
her affection from her husband. Her mindset was to believe that, with
enough sons, she would be enough for Jacob. But after her fourth
son was born, she didn't think about her husband.[4] She simply said,
"This time I will praise the LORD" (Gen. 29:35). She even named
her son Judah, meaning "praise." Instead of naming her expectations,
she simply gave exaltations to God. In the words of Liz Curtis Higgs,
"She decided to praise God for what she had rather than blame him
for what she didn't."[5] Instead of focusing on Jacob's absent affection,
she focused on God's present attention. She knew he was with her in
her lonely circumstances, and she praised him for it.

As a result, she didn't turn herself inside out to make Jacob love her. She knew God saw her and loved her as she was, and that was enough. She dumped all the *shouldities* of what she should be and sang her own life song to God.

"*This time I will praise the* LORD."

I want Leah to have the movie-worthy ending, where Jacob finally sees her as the gift she is. Scripture doesn't tell us if that ever happened. But Leah *did* get a different kind of happily ever after. As time would reveal, Leah's son Judah became an ancestor to David and Jesus. Leah, with the kind eyes and yearning heart, was an important thread in the family tapestry that gave the world Jesus.

At the beginning of her marriage, Leah was forced to muzzle her song and quite literally be someone else. That didn't work out well for anyone, especially Leah. Still, she didn't berate herself for not belonging where she couldn't. While Jacob may have thought Leah wasn't enough, God said she was more than enough.

And so she sang her praise to him.

~Belong Blessing~

May you sense the Lord speaking to you directly and personally today, affirming that you are made in his image and therefore belong in the good place of his own choosing. May you believe in your innermost places that God cannot lie. His words of truth about you—that you are beloved and belong—are all the permission you need to sing your life's song as loud as you like. Let all your *shouldities* be crucified. May you know that God has already scouted your back road and Jesus has traveled it on your behalf, so he is your ever-safe companion as you trek along.

Six

Belonging to Change

A full life and life to the full are two very different things. One is about grasping, the other about receiving. One is about cramming in, the other about room to breathe. One is about striving, the other is about trust. One is about control, the other is about letting go—sometimes for a moment and sometimes for always.

Holley Gerth, *Fiercehearted*

THE CLOCK AND CALENDAR said we were mere minutes into the second day of spring, but we wrapped our arms around one another to fight off the winter chill covering everything.

Your circumstances can do that to you. They can laugh at the seasons as they snatch away your sense of place.

As my kids' friends prepared for spring break trips to snow-packed slopes or sun-drenched beaches or even to stay home and blissfully sleep in, we prepared to go to Oklahoma for the funeral of David's dad. Our hard-working, decade-and-a-half-old minivan could no longer be trusted to get us there, and my smaller car made for tight quarters in the backseat for three teens. So we usually rented a car anytime we made the ten-hour trip that direction. However, given the spring break timing, none could be rented for under $2,000.

Sorry, kiddos, you're going to have to squish all nice and cozy in the backseat of mama's car for this trip.

The heaviness of the trip's purpose squeezed us from all sides.

Really, this trip was déjà vu in its truest sense: only the month before we'd driven to Oklahoma for my own daddy's funeral. My daddy died after a long battle with multiple sclerosis. A sad loss, for certain, but not a shocking one. My father-in-law's own homegoing to heaven was rather unexpected, and our hearts weighed as heavy as a ton of bricks.

Still, we moved ahead, checking off the million to-dos that must be done before leaving for a long trip.

See if the kennel has room for the dog.

Reschedule half a dozen appointments.

Rush through a few loads of laundry.

Get the house key to Aimée so she could feed our kitties and bring in the mail.

We made the familiar drive east across the plains, one we could almost make in our sleep. After time spent recounting memories, hanging with family, and listening to a beautiful funeral service honoring my dear father-in-law, we did a one-eighty and drove west toward Colorado once again.

Making our way on I-70, we joked it was so flat we could see our house three hundred miles before we got there. You can see a lot of things coming miles away, yes. But other things you can't see until they smack you upside the head. What I didn't anticipate this go-around was how the heavyhearted sadness would walk with us long after we walked back through our front door in the Colorado woods.

Personally, these two events were twin bookends to a long, dark winter, but they were also two landmarks of change in our lives on the front lines of several more to come. I grabbed my husband's thick blue-and-green flannel shirt and wore it day after day, wrapping myself in comfort even as I couldn't get warm. Every bit of food went down like sawdust. I stared out the window over and over again, anxious to see hope looking back in.

But life moves on, and routines bring comfort. My daughter needed to be driven to tennis lessons. My sons needed new shoes. My good man needed me to finish my taxes. The pets needed to get their shots. Everyone needed to eat an annoying three times a day.

One evening, a few weeks after we'd returned home, my husband and I went on a date, something we try to do most Friday evenings. Over fish tacos from Salsa Brava's, we had an enjoyable time, and for the first time in a while we found ourselves laughing and feeling more ourselves. We stopped by Lowe's for lightbulbs and a can of spray paint on the way home. (Ah, romance!) We came in through the front door and chatted with the kids about their evening. Then I headed upstairs to change into my jammies, and I decided to check Facebook for the first time that day.

Yeah, that's when everything went south, as I read that a dear writing friend of mine had left a writing group we'd both been a part of for years. I read the post, blinked, and read it again before it liquefied and swam away.

My husband, after coming upstairs and seeing my sorry state, asked what was wrong. I told him we'd lost *two* dads, we had *two* kids graduating high school soon, and now my friend was leaving this writing group. I looked at him, waved my index finger in the air, and said, "And let me just say, this . . . THIS . . . is the final straw!" I shook my head back and forth to a staccato rhythm. "No," I said. "NO. NO. NO. This cannot be. I do *not* accept this!"

He hugged me and smiled weakly, letting out a short laugh.

"I'm so sorry, baby. I guess this may be one of those, 'I reject your reality and substitute my own' moments?"

I nodded my head on his wet shoulder.

Yes, sir. I reject this much change and substitute a little calm familiarity instead, thank you very much. In my mind, I had stood for some time on a rug that was gradually being pulled out from under me. I wobbled but still kept my balance. And then this one last thing threw me completely off-kilter.

It was a little thing, of course. I mean, I'll still talk to this writer-friend all the time. I'll still see her. That particular writing group is still full of fabulous writer-friends. But this last bit of news, in that moment, was too much.

Doesn't it happen like that sometimes? You're hanging on by the calloused ends of your fingertips and then that last bit of pressure makes you let go and lose your mind.

As we can discover, however, often what's bothering us isn't what's *really* bothering us. Something burrows in the dark underneath, and it's that thing we haven't let see the light of day that hinders our belonging. Yes, I was certainly sad I would no longer be able to connect with this writing friend in that group. But when I got down under things, I knew I was upset that, in yet another area of my life, my sense of belonging had changed. I rejected having my belonging place upended with the loss of dear loved ones, the passage of time with my sons graduating, and now this change in a favorite community too.

When we're in a season of change, hope gets buried beneath fifty layers of defeated thinking, and we're sure we need to *do* something to reassure ourselves that we belong. That was me here, repeating *no, no, no* and *this could not would not shall not be.*

I laid down on the bed and exhaled. Instead of refusing to accept the truth or acting like it wasn't so, I let the realities of everything that was slamming into the winter of my heart just sit there next to me. I talked to Jesus and told him out loud, "If you were good before this all happened—which you certainly were—then you're still good today. You still want me to belong today."

And then I sensed him saying in return, *That's right. I do want you to belong today. That hasn't and will not ever change. These life changes mean you must travel a different road to get to your belonging place, but it's still there.*

This is the thing I continually forget about where I belong and with whom: it will change.

• • •

If you've read my previous book, *Girl Meets Change*, you know I had a longtime difficult relationship with change. You know I saw it as a hindrance to my happiness, a roadblock to my contentment and peace. While I've learned to look for the good in change, found at the intersection where my anxiety over it meets God's purpose found in it, I still struggle when that change removes my belonging in one way or another. I panic and believe the way things are today will be the way they are forever. I'm overcome with the thought, *I hope you enjoyed belonging here for the time you did, little lady. Because that's gone and you'll never have it again.*

The enemy is as mean as a snake, but he's not stupid. He's an expert at capitalizing on your loss, showing you all the ways change alters your sense of belonging for the worst, always and forever.

But that's not true—not true at all.

Not long ago, a dear friend of mine reminded me that death always brings some kind of reconciliation. Jesus's death on the cross reconciled us with God, always and forever. Death always brings resurrection too. A rising up of something that is better for us, because Jesus is always *for* us and *with* us through every change and sense of removed belonging we encounter.

So now I begin to look in my life for what will be raised up from these losses and changes. Is there something I can look forward to that couldn't make itself visible till now?

If God is still good today, and he wants me to belong somewhere, then when I'm ready I need to pack up my courage and explore that new back road. On the way, I'll sense a reconciliation by way of a growth in my belonging place. And even as I mourn the passing of my dad and dad-in-law, I rejoice in receiving extended time to connect with family and circle around memories of these beloved men. Just relishing these moments alone strengthens the foundation my feet stand upon.

I also find myself growing into my belonging place as told in Deuteronomy 29:29:

> The secret things belong to the LORD our God, but the things that are revealed belong to us and to our children forever, that we may do all the words of this law.

While God holds the right to be able to keep things secret this side of heaven, he also reveals things to us. His Holy Spirit speaks to our hearts, telling us things we couldn't possibly know on our own. He shares things for our own edification and for the edification of our children, for the blessing of others in our circles of influence. And one of those things is how his road to our belonging place is always best for us, but it will often not look the way we think it should. It will hold directional changes we didn't see coming. But, as I've learned the hard way, sometimes we need to give up the familiar what *is* for a better what *will be*.

If God was good before your change, then he is good today. May we stay in step with the Holy Spirit, letting his nudges and whispers lead us on. Yeah, when change takes us down unfamiliar roads, those roads will still lead us to God.

And that will never change.

traveling companion:
CONNIE

Connie, a wife and a mom of three sons, homeschooled her children and also taught other kiddos at a study center she established. As an active member of her church and community, she enjoyed playing in an orchestra and getting together with friends. Ever a good listener,

Connie was the kind of friend who stood with her people through their highs and lows. While health problems popped up for Connie every once in a while, they were minor, not chronic or life-altering in any significant way.

In 2005, all that changed when Connie went skiing and tore her ACL. She had surgery to repair the tear, but stress from the surgery triggered her autoimmune diseases (Lupus and Sjogren's) and caused her body to spiral downward. First came a blood clot. Then came inflammation, not only in her knee but everywhere else too. The inflammation and ensuing arthritis became so severe that Connie couldn't pull laundry from the dryer without extreme discomfort.

That might have been the end to her story: dealing with chronic pain as many people do. But over the summer, Connie also developed a painful rash of sores from head to toe. Her dermatologist tried several different medicines, but nothing helped. In fact, the final treatment her dermatologist tried caused Connie to lose her hair. Having the persistent rash was bad enough, but losing her hair—a strong part of a woman's femininity—marked a real low point for Connie. Not only that, she struggled with thoughts that her enduring health changes would remove her from her belonging within her community and her family. She thought, *Will my loved ones be embarrassed to be seen with me and my rash in public? Am I less valuable to my community because of my limitations and what I look like?*

Finally, Labor Day weekend of that year, her blood platelet level suddenly and inexplicably dropped. Her nose started bleeding and wouldn't stop. After she began bleeding elsewhere too, her husband took her to the ER. There they learned that while a healthy person has around 150,000–400,000 platelets of blood, tests showed Connie's levels at 2,000. With Connie's life hanging on a thin line, her doctors placed her in the ICU. It was at this low point that Connie's doctors found an experimental treatment that began the healing process and put her on a path to remission.

As Connie's body improved with medication, she moved to a recovery room. During the week she spent there, she read Jeremiah

Burroughs's *The Rare Jewel of Christian Contentment* and Scripture. People visited, and friends brought pizza. Connie had been so sick she almost lost her life, but she remembers that week fondly. When it came time to leave the hospital, she felt a little sad because it had been a sweet, concentrated time of Jesus coming alongside her, meeting her and helping her.

During the darkest days of the rash and hair loss, Connie clung to Lamentations 3:19–25 like the lifeline it is. In this passage, the prophet Jeremiah says,

> Remember my affliction and my wanderings,
>   the wormwood and the gall!
> My soul continually remembers it
>   and is bowed down within me.
> But this I call to mind,
>   and therefore I have hope:
>
> The steadfast love of the LORD never ceases,
>   his mercies never come to an end;
> they are new every morning;
>   great is your faithfulness.
> "The LORD is my portion," says my soul,
>   "therefore I will hope in him."
>
> The LORD is good to those who wait for him.

My soul . . . is bowed down . . . but this I call to mind, and therefore I have hope.

Those were down days for Connie, days when she didn't want to do anything. However, she hugged these verses close because in them Jeremiah acknowledged the hard *and* the hope. Connie knew it was okay to lament her troubles because she still landed on the truth: God is faithful, and because she belonged to him, he would faithfully see her through this trial.

Connie also learned that while she worried this life-altering change would remove her sense of belonging with her loved ones, it actually affirmed it. When she attended the final dinner at her sons' Boy Scout camp, her family wasn't embarrassed to be seen with her at all. When she went to church each Sunday and saw her friends out and about, they didn't treat her any differently. Not only did her husband stand by her and care for her and their family during her illness, he let her know her beauty far outlasted any illness or hardship. Other people might've noticed the rash and given her a second glance here or there, but all in all Connie felt the Lord sheltering her from what those reactions could've been. The people who mattered treated her as they always had. Connie experienced a focused time of feeling loved on by God and others. God's daily mercies showed up in a hundred small, kind gestures, all affirming where she belonged within her place and people.

Since that time, Connie has learned her disease is actually an autoimmune disease that mimics lupus, and with that new diagnosis comes new symptoms and struggles. But those struggles don't include an absence of place or people. Keeping in mind Galatians 6:2, which calls us to bear one another's burdens, Connie is open with others about her struggles. In turn, they find her a safe person to share their own struggles with. And in that give-and-take, all find a renewed sense of belonging.[1]

~Belong Blessing~

If your change has you taking a new road to your belonging place, may you know the words of Isaiah 43:19 are for you: Jesus is doing a new thing, making a way for you through the wild wilderness and a river through the dusty, barren desert. Before you see the way, may you hold the hand of the Way as he travels with you on your back road. May God bring you people who speak life into you as you walk this changing season. May your eyes stay open to your belonging place and your people there, and may your heart be open to God's good found in your days.

Part II

Finding

Looking in all the right places.

Seven

Growing in the Dark

Give it time. God is at work underground. Quit trying to force fruit that's not yet due.

Beth Moore

WHEN UNWELCOME CHANGE TRIGGERS that *outsider* feeling, we need to remember God still grows good things within us. But as we walk down the dreaded new path, we may be frustrated because while we know these truths, we just don't feel them. What we know on the inside isn't yet visible on the outside. We want to see the evidence of good things growing in this new season, namely a more settled-in belonging place. But right now, it's hard to see in the dark of the here and now.

In the winter months, the tall aspens, cottonwoods, and maples don't change aboveground. Their naked branches stick out through the long months and do not transform or grow. However, their roots can change, experiencing slow growth while the top remains completely dormant.

Unlike the aboveground parts of most trees that pass the winter in a prolonged dormancy—marked by unbroken inactivity until spring—tree roots seem to maintain a readiness to grow independent of the aboveground parts of the tree. That is, roots remain mostly inactive but can and do function and grow during winter months whenever soil temperatures are favorable, even if the air aboveground is brutally cold.[1]

Could it be, in those dark times of change, when we long to belong in a larger place but see no evidence of growth there, that the growth is moving in a downward direction? That growth is happening where roots reach and spread and become stronger?

Yes, because growth still happens in the dark, and good things grow from lowly, dark places.

Faith is being certain of what we do not see, and nature echoes this all around us. We don't see what the poppies and peonies do below ground, but we have faith that something is going on. When springtime comes and we see small shoots pushing through the stubborn earth, our faith is rewarded. If nothing ever happened below ground, we'd miss out on the show in our flower boxes and beds. More often than not, it takes time for our faith to reveal outcomes. Like the earth, perhaps we too need to rest in that colder, darker season.

But when I'm lonely, afraid, or tired of the way things are, I don't remember this.

Those who know me know winter is my least favorite season, which is mighty unfortunate since I live in Colorado, where winter lasts thirteen months. Ish. Usually, I find each new winter charming and idyllic, at least at first. I mean, what's more magical than Christmas in the wooded pines of a mountain town? What's more delightful than January days spent cozy by the fire? I eat up all the sublime winter festivities like snow ice cream. But come April and May, when the heavy snowstorms have long since worn out their welcome, I'm decidedly less fired up about the long season.

This past winter, however, I put on my big girl pants and decided to change my attitude. Spurred on by the fact that I had two children graduating high school in the spring, I decided I would not wish away winter. I would slow down and relax through the season, to see what gifts it offers that I normally don't care to find.

The winter months, it turns out, possess a slower rhythm than the other seasons. Taking a cue from nature, I too rested for a prolonged period of time. I don't mean I took naps every day or ignored real-life responsibilities. Honestly, this past winter was part of the busiest, most demanding year our family has experienced thus far. I mean I actually relaxed into the place God had me at that time. In spite of single-digit temps, I bundled up and took winter walks. I refilled our busy bird feeders. I read book after book in front of our woodstove. I cooked enough soup and desserts to make my three teens praise me at the city gates—or in the high school hallways, at least. (Cooking for teens covers over a multitude of arguments, slammed doors, and angsty moods. Ask me how I know.) I did nothing extraordinary; I just relaxed in my place by enjoying all those little things rather than breathlessly moving on to the next thing.

I know that complaining about the weather is a luxury. Our circumstances can be so much bigger and more serious than chilly temperatures overstaying their welcome. This same winter, my dad and my husband's dad both passed away. Other hard things happened that I haven't discussed publicly, things that also required grief to have a presence in our lives. But just the same, not wishing it all away was one small way I didn't let my circumstances rob me of the rest found in my current belonging place. It was one small way I drew near to Christ, affirming that he who gives of himself in a thousand different ways is lighting the way for us to belong in the dark.

• • •

As I ponder this idea of steadfastly drawing near to Christ in dark seasons, I think about a particular passage of Scripture, when Jesus drew near to two disciples shortly after his resurrection. These two men, knee-deep in conversation, were talking about all that had happened concerning Jesus, including his death and the reports of the empty tomb. It seemed all hope had been lost with Jesus's death—the darkness surrounded all those who thought Jesus had come to redeem Israel. These men wanted to believe the reports that Jesus was alive, but their belief sputtered because they had not seen Jesus with their own eyes.

They couldn't take their eyes off what they *had* seen—Jesus's brutal death—and needed stronger evidence to convince them Jesus was alive.[2] Jesus walked near them, and although they conversed with him for a while, their eyes were kept from recognizing him (Luke 24:13–35).

After inviting Jesus to lodge with them for the night, they sat at the table together and watched as he took the bread, blessed it, and broke it before sharing it. At that moment, they recognized Jesus—and just as they recognized him, Jesus vanished from their sight. Undoubtedly slack-jawed that this man was Jesus and not a stranger, they asked each other, "Didn't we feel on fire as he conversed with us on the road?" (Luke 24:32 Message).

Encountering Jesus will do that: it will decimate the darkness as it ignites your heart with the fire of Hope. It will bring you purpose and identity, especially while traveling through dark places.

But I find that when I'm in a dark season of wanting that elusive belonging place, I am one of those travelers on the road to Emmaus, absentmindedly dragging my heart along to wherever I'm going. Jesus walks beside me just as assuredly as during any other season, but my eyes remain blind to him because I struggle to believe he could really be there. I struggle to take my eyes off the sadness of not belonging where I want to belong and with whom I want to belong. I struggle to remember this season is purposefully slow, yes, but also purposefully abundant in its own way.

Lord, in my own season of growing down, open my eyes to all the ways you have me in a place of abundance today.

Because the night is bright as day to him, he doesn't need the light to do his good work. He can work in the small, the hidden, the ink-black dark. And in those things he is working to grow us through this season toward a greater belonging place.

When we don't see much changing aboveground, we can keep our own soil favorable by drawing closer to God, knowing in this season he's asking us to strengthen our roots by allowing him to affirm our belonging from the inside out. Each of us can ask ourselves, *What helps me feel close to God? How can I renew by growing down? How can I draw near to Christ so I can relax in him and remain content where God has me today?*

Of course, what works for each of us is different. For me, these questions are best asked and answered while taking a walk. Surrounding myself with God's creation helps me see myself not as excessively important or hopelessly insignificant. It helps me see myself as I really am: one God sees and knows.

There's something about being outside that makes it easier to see what's beautiful around us—and how we beautifully fit into God's creation.

More than that, nature offers nurturing solitude. A study of Finnish teens showed that when they went into natural settings after upsetting events, they could clear their minds, gain perspective, and relax there.[3] God walked through Eden in the cool of the day, and our own Edens await exploration around us too.

What we can do dailyish in these dark seasons is find where we best relax and recharge. Maybe we go there for an hour a day, or for a fifteen-minute break, or just long enough to shut the bathroom door without the kids finding us. I think the moments do regularly show up; we just have to be mindful about using them wisely.

The specifics of how we relax in this growing down season aren't important. Using the time and not wasting it is. This is not the time to fret about growing up or out to be seen in our belonging place. This is the season to be known by growing down, to build a stronger sense of belonging that is rooted in Christ, in whom our closeness overshadows our place here on earth.

I'm a chronic window stare-outer, and one of my favorite subjects of observation is our trio of bird feeders off our side porch. All the livelong day, chickadees dart, dance, and prance among the feeders and pine branches. They're our constant companions in the winter.

Recently, I learned these black-capped chickadees each weigh the same as two nickels in your hand. Their brain memory centers grow bigger and bigger, beginning in late summer. Each bird's hippocampus swells as its neurons increase to record a precise map of its half-mile range of terrain, an X of sorts marking each bit of tree bark or log crack where it's tucked a seed.[4] Each chickadee has thousands of them in secret hiding places, a connect-the-dots game of survival during the long, dark winter nights. As it eats up its seeds, its map and hippocampus shrink. If things go as they should, each chickadee's cache outlasts the snow and cold.[5]

Chickadees make calling sounds in the winter to let their partner or flock-mates know where they are. However, they don't sing till spring.[6] In their brains, the centers that control how they give voice to songs diminish in the winter. They don't sing often because they don't need to this time of year. But as the little bird's internal map shrinks as winter moves into spring, other parts of its brain expand; the bird resumes singing in springtime, to woo a mate or announce its territory, as these control centers of its brain enliven.[7] It's just one way God allowed these tiny creatures' brains to be able to conserve energy.

It's as if God tells even the smallest of creatures, *There's a time to take inventory, and a time to sing.* Perhaps what's good for one of God's tiniest creations is good for us too. Sometimes growth stalls in one area to allow room for growth in another.

There is a time to learn about yourself before the song comes within the longer light of spring. There is a time to grow down and take inventory of the good things around you today by leaning into Christ as he reveals more of himself to you, including more about where you belong.

We may not be able to see it, but good things grow in the dark. Let's give ourselves the gift of time for God to do his good work in the light . . . and in the dark.

Spring—and its fruit—will come.

traveling companion:
AUNDREA

As a general rule, Aundrea made friends easily in life. She'd been through more than her fair share of long-distance moves, so "starting over" and meeting new people became routine for her. However, all that changed after a cross-country move from Ohio to California with her husband and two young daughters. During that period, Aundrea had a long "growing down" season that included few friends. Struggling to belong within her new community, she spent a good deal of time asking God why she couldn't seem to connect with anyone beyond basic pleasantries. No direct answers came for a long, dark time. However, the Lord showed her other meaningful discoveries in that winter season of growing down, including:

> A deepened relationship with the Lord, where she relied on him to minister to her needs rather than other people.
>
> Time for herself and some much-needed soul searching to work on issues she'd ignored for most of her adult life.
>
> Choosing friends with wisdom rather than running to any group and talking to the first woman she met with kids the same age as hers.
>
> Much more intentional time with her husband and kids that has grown their relationships exponentially.

With time, Aundrea did meet people with whom she felt she belonged, and she was able to have richer friendships because she came to those relationships with a healthier self. Not only that, but the Lord expanded her view of looking for friendships in women she didn't normally gravitate toward, women who may not have kids of similar ages to hers or share her interests. She learned to pay better attention and value people for more than similarity.

Aundrea grew down in this darker season, and that growing down looked like a richer relationship with the Lord, processing through lifelong questions, and time with family that was pure gold. She learned to lean more on Christ and her husband. She developed a true contentment in her belonging with them, something she wouldn't trade for anything.[8]

~Belong Blessing~

When frustrations settle near because it's too dark to see where you belong, remember you are growing toward your place. It's simply hidden in the dark. May you accept it will stay hidden until the time arrives for it to be revealed. When you're discouraged because your perceived lack of growth feels like God may be distant, may you remember that, like snow-covered winter soil, we are covered with his mercy and presence always. May you rest under his hand, patiently believing that if you care to make good things grow, God cares and moves all the more to make good things grow. Our Savior Jesus grew within the dark place of his ordinary mother's womb before he became visible to the outside world. May you make a space to discover what good God is growing for your belonging place in your season of growing down.

eight

Eating Well

Christ is the only one who when people spent time with him, the more sinless they found him to be. It's the opposite for us people.

Lee Strobel

As is our practice every sixish months, my daughter Faith found herself in the dentist's chair for her biannual teeth cleaning. Neither one of us have a great love for the dentist. (The place, that is. We really like our dentist the person!) This is mostly because, for us, dentist visits equal pain. I don't have stellar enamel and neither does my husband. Our girl inherited a double portion of bad teeth genetics, so she's especially susceptible to cavities and other fun stuff involving needles and extractions. Her awareness of all this means our girl is hypervigilant about taking care of her teeth. She cleans her pearly whites with more intention than most doctors clean their hands before surgery. Brushing for two minutes, swishing mouthwash, and flossing daily. She does it all.

On this particular day, I assumed this dental cleaning would be easy breezy as there were no specific teeth problems on her horizon.

Yeah, I assumed wrong.

It began well enough—Faith and the dental hygienist, whom we'd never met before, engaged in small talk. Since Faith was quite young at the time, I went with her but sat in the corner of the room and flipped through an outdated issue of *In Style* magazine. I listened passively to their conversation, but my ears perked up when she asked Faith, "So are you brushing your teeth, Faith?"

Faith emphatically shook her head yes.

The hygienist looked toward me with narrowed eyes.

"It's true," I responded, setting the magazine on my lap. "She brushes more diligently than most adults." I made a joke with the hygienist that while Faith took good care of her teeth, she'd likely find a different story where Faith's brothers were concerned.

She looked back down at my daughter and responded, "Well, let's just see how right you and your mom are, shall we?"

I looked back down at the magazine, furrowing my brows at her dramatic tone.

She then poked around Faith's teeth and called me over to see a spot Faith's toothbrush consistently missed. I nodded, more than willing to accept my nine-year-old still had room for improvement in caring for her teeth. But since Ms. Hygienist said the majority of Faith's teeth looked just fine, I went back to my chair and assumed we'd move on.

Yeah, strike two for me.

The hygienist continued to peck at Faith's teeth with instruments while pecking at her toothbrushing habits with her pointed words. The lecture went on and on *and on*. After what seemed like hours, the hygienist concluded the exam and proceeded to brush and floss Faith's teeth with such vigor I wondered if she suspected Faith of holding government secrets. It's then I noticed the wet corners of Faith's closed eyes.

The hygienist must have seen them too, because she scoffed impatiently, "Now, Faith, no need to cry. I'm barely touching you!"

Cue Mama Bear tossing the magazine to the floor next to my chair and sitting up tall. I didn't care about maintaining some level of propriety or not making a scene or not hurting her feelings. I wanted this lady to back off, and I wanted her to back off pronto.

"You know what?" I said, leaning in. "While I'm certain this isn't your intention, you are clearly doing more than 'barely touching her.' She needs a lighter touch and a more gracious tone from you, and she needs it *now*."

Insert uncomfortable silence here.

Great day, there's nothing more fun than a self-righteous dental hygienist, especially one who seems to get a kick out of criticizing and shaming you for not perfectly caring for your teeth—as if perfect was possible. More often than not, my hygienists have been kind, gentle, and nonjudgmental people. I *adore* our current hygienists. (Hat tip, Powers Dental Group!) But along the way, there have been a couple who seem to imply, "You'll never belong in the Gold Star Brushing Club, dearie, no matter what you do." Now, I don't really want or need to be in that club, but still. The barrage of criticism isn't fun.

Isn't the same thing true with our enemy, Satan? He will find a hidden or obvious flaw, then point it out to you again and again and again. He'll go on and on about it and exploit the flaw by bossing you, criticizing you, and shaming you into believing that flaw keeps you from belonging.

He will work through others to accomplish this, sometimes in a "Gotcha!" way of communicating. When you start to cry, he'll hit you from the other direction. *Hey, you don't have it that bad. Only wimps cry over this stuff.*

We talked before about how we need to listen to Jesus's affirmations to us rather than the enemy's accusations about us so we keep our mindset in its proper belonging place. The enemy, you see, can never be reasoned with. Negotiating with him—the original terrorist—is not an option. However, I don't always try to negotiate with him. Sometimes I just straight up agree with him.

If I stand up to pushy dental hygienists, why don't I stand up to him? Yes, we're flawed and sinful—none of us have our act together all the time. Some of us are sure we never do (hand up!). There's a gaping abyss between each of us and God, and we all need Jesus to cross it. But can we just be kind to ourselves by not agreeing with the nonsense the enemy hurls at us? Can we just sit up tall and say, "You need to back off, and you need to back off now"? In the words of Romans 8:1, there is no (none, zilch, nada) condemnation for those who are in Christ Jesus. He walked across that abyss by dying on the cross for us to bring us in.

So we don't dine on unhealthy thoughts, words, or actions. We don't throw our hands up in resignation and say, "I will always be out." We dine on the Word of Life and throw the enemy off of his self-righteous, self-erected throne.

• • •

When you and I are on the outside looking in, the cure is to *keep looking in*. However, we need to be mindful of where we're looking in. A good place to always begin is looking in God's Word.

If we want to keep our soil favorable by becoming more rooted in Christ, it's paramount to be in the Word on a regular basis. When we regularly open the pages of Scripture to feast on the Bread of Life, we discover a meal of goodness the Lord wants to use to feed our hearts in very personal ways. We discover the most accurate picture of ourselves and our place in this world.

Reading Scripture is the surest back road way to belonging, to remaining in Christ and relaxing into God's plan for each of us. It's how we internalize his truth rather than the wonky truth we tell ourselves. It's how we let God have the final say this minute, this hour, this day rather than the cranky, critical Other Voices. Reading God's Word acts as the barbed-wire fence keeping the enemy's ugly lies about our belonging far away from us. It turns his pointed words back on himself.

And it's the way we internalize this idea that God has a belonging place for us, because we are not the exception to the rule. One of his promises is "God makes a home for the lonely" (Ps. 68:6 NASB). He has a place for each of us with people who value and respect us.

On a practical level, looking in God's Word might resemble investigating Scripture in the most traditional of "quiet times." Or it might look like flipping through Scripture notecards while going on a walk or sitting in the carpool line. Or it may look like immersing ourselves in nature and meditating on God's Word within his created world. It might look like pouring a cup of tea or coffee as the accompaniment to our reading. No one gets to boss us into what that time should look like. It's strictly between each of us and God, done in a way that makes sense for us within our schedule and life.

The Word is living, and through it God speaks and gives life to us. But we need to turn down the static invading our exterior and interior life so we can make a space to hear what God wants to say.

The other day, I read a verse tucked in John 8 that made my eyes grow big and my heart burst like a firecracker. Jesus, speaking to a group of Jewish listeners, said, "You seek to kill me because my word finds no place in you" (v. 37).

If I want God's Word to find a place within me—and I surely do—then I need to spend time with it, taking it in.

We don't read the Word because that's what we know we're supposed to do. We read the Word because it makes the enemy back off, and it makes him back off *now*.

We read the Word and remember we don't belong under Satan's accusations. We belong under God's affirmations. Yes, God will convict, but his convictions are always served on a plate of love with a side of grace. We will forever leave his company feeling full on what he gives rather than starved for what has been taken. God's conviction and direction will be *for* us, and once we've turned them over, examined them, and let them do good work in our lives, the change they bring will make us feel lighter, happier, and more secure in our belonging place.

Do you feel lost? God's Word is your compass to get back on track.

Do you feel forgotten? God's Word will be where you're seen and known.

Do you feel unlovable and beyond help? God's Word will move you to the center of hope.

Do you think you've screwed up too much? God's Word will give you unlimited fresh do-overs.

Do you believe you don't deserve to belong? God's Word will show you how and where you do.

Don't worry about the logistics of getting it done. Just deliberately open the calendar, open the book, and open your heart. Enjoy the time. *Enjoy him.*

Because he enjoys you.

traveling companion:
KELLI

Kelli's husband, Shawn, had a fun-loving and easygoing nature about him that drew people together and created community wherever he went.[1] Still, he was a US Marine through and through, and in him beat the heart of a warrior. Whether caring for his family or his fellow Marines, he wanted his people to be content and happy, and he did what he could to make that a reality. He poured his heart into people out of a genuine care for them.[2] Shawn loved others well, and his presence left any environment better than it was before.

The fifteenth year of Shawn and Kelli's marriage found them stationed in Hawaii—paradise by anyone's definition. On January 15, 2016, Kelli and her four children kissed Shawn goodbye before he headed out for a routine nighttime training mission. As Kelli drifted off to sleep that night, she listened to the sounds of his squadron's helicopters flying overhead.

Later that night, Kelli's worst nightmare came to life. Shawn and eleven other Marines died in a helicopter crash off Oahu's North Shore. Kelli lost her loving husband and helpmate, and her four children lost their devoted dad.

With time, other losses also became visible, like Kelli's sense of belonging within the military community at large.

Kelli wrote,

> Every move I ever made in my adult life was because the US Marine Corps told me to. Shawn got orders for when, where and how long, and I gladly followed him for 15 years. But in the blink of an eye, I was cut loose. I've experienced incredible support from my US Marine Corps family. I know we will always be a part of them, but it's just not the same. . . . Being a widow is isolating and lonely for anyone, but as a military widow, I had this whole past life that only another military spouse can understand.[3]

Between planning children's birthday parties and her husband's memorial, Kelli packed up her Hawaii house and moved her family to be near her parents in Kansas.

In certain ways, losing her beloved husband meant Kelli's heart would never finish breaking. But on the first day following the crash and onward—as she maneuvered the new task of learning to become a civilian again—the sharp stab of loss's pain met the sharp awareness of Christ's presence. When there were no words because the loss made no sense, Kelli discovered words of Truth were the only thing that did make sense. So her friends read Scripture to her and sent her verses the Lord put on their hearts. Rather than allow easy "fix-it" statements or clichés to do the work for them, they knew it was wise to send God's words before their own.[4]

Kelli said these verses, sent via texts, notes, and phone calls, have been manna for her day and God's way of letting her know he sees her. Sometimes Kelli would receive two or three different messages with the same verse on the same day, and it was abundantly clear what message God wanted her to know. Kelli knows she's seen.

Today Kelli is a speaker and board member for Folds of Honor, a nonprofit organization that works to provide educational opportunities via financial aid to families of fallen or wounded American soldiers. Within this organization, Kelli has found a renewed purpose: passing on hope to other families experiencing their greatest fear come true and the subsequent loss of belonging because of it.

Sometimes the worst possible thing happens to make someone lose her belonging place—in more ways than one. Dining on the Bread of Life brings God's peace about the unknown future near. Because when the unexplainable happens, only the peace of God that surpasses all understanding can help us walk forward into our new belonging place.

~Belong Blessing~

Whether that critical Other Voice is in your head or your hamlet, may you hear God's voice loudest of all. May the Lord show you where to open up space in your day to hang out with him so you can make a space in yourself for his Word. May that space remain uncluttered by distractions and expectations as you simply receive God's affirmations in your belonging place.

nine

Looking in the Quiet

When I begin the day with God's Word, with silence, with
a grounding sense of his love for me, then I find it's easier to
bring those things with me throughout the day, and it's harder
for me to locate them if I didn't pause with them at the start.

Shauna Niequist, *Savor*

BEFORE ANYONE OUTSIDE OF CENTRAL TEXAS ever heard of
a shiplap-loving, pixie-dust-throwing woman named Joanna Gaines,
Joanna dreamed of opening a small boutique home décor store in her
hometown of Waco, Texas. With encouragement from her husband,
Chip, Joanna opened the store, called Magnolia, and enjoyed its success. After a time, however, she closed Magnolia because she felt the
Lord calling her to stay home and raise her two young children. She
was somewhat sad to do so—she loved putting her creative skills to
work through her store. But she had peace with that decision because
she also sensed the Lord telling her that if she would trust him with
her dreams, he would take them further than she imagined.[1]

Sometime later, after their HGTV show *Fixer Upper* began, Chip and Joanna were enjoying a vacation in Arizona when they stopped at a beautiful garden. Chip encouraged Joanna to take an hour or so within the garden to just reflect on the past year and let God speak to her about what the following year might look like. It was in the garden that Joanna felt the Lord say it was time to reopen her little Magnolia store. She was hesitant and thought, *No, I don't think I can do it*. But he quietly told her again, *It's time.*[2]

A few months later, Joanna reopened Magnolia. If you follow the Gaines's story at all, you know this turned into Magnolia Market, a sizable home, garden, and lifestyle shopping complex in downtown Waco. My daughter and I visited there a couple years ago, and it's as magical and delightful as we thought it would be.

You and I may never be able to relate to Joanna's wild success and huge following, but there is something we can learn from her story: goodness comes from listening to and heeding God's voice in the quiet, even when he asks us to make a change or accept a new direction that takes us from a place we already feel we belong. Even when obeying him makes us a little sad, hesitant, scared, or just plain twitchy about what might come next.

After her own season of growing down by investing in her family, Joanna showed she belonged on the larger platform God told her he'd give. But first she had to intentionally travel the back road way of placing herself in a quiet spot to hear his voice.

You may be one who hears God's voice audibly or, like me, you may be one who senses him speaking to your heart more than your ears. Either way, the quiet place allows you to tune your heart and soul to his voice. It allows you to listen for how and where he may be directing you toward community or opening your eyes to the people you already have around you.

Of course, when we plant ourselves in the living and active Word of God, we plant ourselves in his presence. But in this busy, noisy world in which we live, it's also important for each of us to experience the Lord's presence in a quiet space. Not necessarily a completely silent space but a *quiet* one. Within this space, we can hear what God says to not only affirm our belonging but direct us toward the people with whom and the places in which he desires us to fit.

Where do you feel best set up—in the most practical of ways—to hear from the Lord?

Depending on the day and your schedule, the answer probably changes. Garden spots and gazebos near the ocean make dreamy locales, but more often than not our quiet place looks like the well-worn corner of the sofa, the canned tomato section of aisle 5 at the grocery store, or the driver's seat of your car as you wait for your kiddo's practice to finish.

You might exercise that spiritual habit of taking a walk or a nap or a loop around the home section of Target and sense his presence and direction just the same.

● ● ●

Other than sitting my hind end down and reading Scripture, spending time listening to the Lord in the quiet is the chief way I lasso anxiety over belonging struggles. It's the most helpful thing in banishing my panic monsters. You know what I'm talking about, don't you? Those little ogres, the devil's minions, that take you from 0–120 mph when something happens—or doesn't happen. Those awful creatures that answer every *what if* question with the worst-case scenario.

These panic monsters are more familiar with my home address than I wish.

One evening, my son James planned to attend a local school play with a friend. A couple hours before he was to leave, the weather turned awful—mammoth snowflakes fell down in sheets and stuck to the roads. The school holding the play was a good thirty minutes away in good weather, let alone bad weather with slick roads.

My husband, David, tried the roads first, and he decided that if James took it slowly, he should be just fine. Sure enough, James arrived to the school safe and sound.

After enjoying the show, James texted David and me to say he was leaving. We told him we'd see him when he got home, which should've been about forty-five minutes from then.

When forty-five minutes came and went, I didn't worry. But when another forty-five went by with still no James, I made the only logical conclusion.

Clearly, my son was dead on the side of the road.

Cue a full-on, no-holds-barred parenting panic.

My husband, ever steady and levelheaded, calmly put on his heavy boots and started down the road in the direction James had gone. And that's when we both saw car lights coming our way. I held my breath till I saw my son's handsome, brown-haired head peek out of his rolled-down window.

Then I promptly buried my head in my hands and cried my eyes out.

It turns out James—along with eight other people—had gotten stuck in a snowdrift, and he'd immediately set out to find help in getting unstuck. Relieved he was okay, I only gave him an abbreviated lecture on checking in with ol' Mom and Dad *first* the next time something like that happened.

I mean, have mercy on our stressed-out, ever-loving selves.

I know sometimes we have our most dreaded fears realized. The doorbell chimes with the worst news. The phone rings with the scary diagnosis confirmed. The email confirms an opportunity lost. Still, I would venture to believe that more often than not, the worst thing does *not* happen. Oh, in our head it does. The panic monsters rub their hands in glee because they know they get to run roughshod over us like some shoot-'em-up cowboy movie villain. In a thousand awful ways, they grab us by the arm and make us sprint down our own back road to a no-good destination. They push us into the front row at our child's imaginary funeral. They run a movie through our mind showing us all that could go wrong.

Spending time in the quiet is how we sit on the panic monsters. Checking in with our Dad in heaven *first* is one way we rest more and worry less about where we are today.

It's where we find mercy for our stressed-out, maxed-out selves.

When it comes to where I belong, my head and heart have a lot of experience at confirming my worst fears too.

You used to have what it takes to belong here, Kristen, but not anymore.

Too bad you said that stupid thing. Now you're out.

Of course they didn't pick you. Why would anyone pick you?

They didn't invite you because you don't have the moxie to hang with them. You don't have what it takes.

You know what? I don't have what it takes to belong where I'm not supposed to belong. That just means it's not God's best for me. God is faithful and will show me where I'm supposed to belong.

If we need to mourn a sense of loss in our belonging place, then by all means, let the tears come. No need to push them away or cover them up. We can let them drive us to prayer, not panic. Our prayers pave our back roads to belonging. Looking in the quiet helps us take it slow and relax in Christ by hearing his voice first, not the panic monsters.

Recently, I read in the book *Sacred Parenting* by Gary Thomas a beautiful description that gave me a helpful visual for keeping my emotions in check. While the passage is geared toward emotions regarding parenting, his imagery here speaks to a wide range of circumstances.

> I have to step back . . . and take inventory. I have to put my emotions to the test and corral them with my intellect. I don't ignore them, but neither should I allow them to drive my reaction. They're just there, like the weather, making the situation more or less pleasant, but they must not determine what I do.[3]

Our emotions should get a seat at the table; we should acknowledge and not ignore them. But like the weather, they are part of the situation, not the definition of it. Sitting with the Lord in the quiet is equivalent to watching weather reports: it prepares us to handle what is to come. It helps us know where we should be and how to set ourselves up for success with our people.

To help me pray more and panic less, I whisper this verse-prayer: "Help me take every thought captive to you."

I do it in the quiet of my day—over the kitchen sink, under the pine trees as I walk, on the front walkway as I wave goodbye to one of my sons behind the steering wheel.

I do it to practice belonging where I am. In the quiet of the morning or the still of the evening or the calm-before-the-storm of the 3:15 carpool line, God shows me how I'm where I'm supposed to be, with the people I'm supposed to be with.

> GOD is fair and just;
> He corrects the misdirected,
> Sends them in the right direction.
>
> He gives the rejects his hand,
> And leads them step-by-step.
>
> From now on every road you travel
> Will take you to GOD.
> Follow the Covenant signs;
> Read the charted directions. (Ps. 25:8–10 Message)

From now on every road you travel will take you to God, and God always wants you to belong.

Let him take you to your back road to belonging instead of the panic monsters taking you to Nowheresville. "Be still before the LORD and wait patiently for him" (Ps. 37:7).

Let's say no to the panic monsters by saying yes to the quiet. And let's say yes to enjoying the goodness that comes from listening to God's voice in the quiet, moving us toward prayer and peace.

May we take the time to stop, be still, and listen.

traveling companions:
THE ISRAELITES

With their sense of place threatened, the Israelites were guilty of doing what we are often also guilty of doing: looking side to side for help rather than looking up. With their emotions firmly out of control, they panicked and rushed to act out of their own understanding rather than wait, pray, and lean on the Lord's understanding.

In Isaiah 30, the prophet tells of a scene short on hope and high on hysteria. The Israelites' neighbors, the Assyrians, looked to expand their empire toward Israel, and Israel—God's own beloved—panicked. Instead of stilling themselves before the Lord to wait for his directives, they turned to their neighbor Egypt for help. Instead of looking up to God for aid, they looked over to Egypt for their salvation.

God spoke through Isaiah with the simplest back road route to peace when their belonging was threatened. "In returning and rest you shall be saved; in quietness and in trust shall be your strength. But you were unwilling, and you said, 'No!'" (Isa. 30:15–16).

Return to rest, quietness, and trust. It requires so little from us, yet we say no thanks and instead grasp for our own flimsy control. We turn our own way instead of God's way. In varying degrees, doing so only leads to our destruction.

Without spending time listening for the Lord's direction and affirmation, we're susceptible to looking to other people to fill us up in ways no human can do. It's imperative to intentionally spend time looking to God to do what only he can: fill us up as he leads us to our belonging place. Like any parent can tell you, God delights in comforting and helping his kids. How it must grieve him to stand with us, ready to help, but in one way or another we tell him no thanks. We put our belonging in the hands of another, believing he or she can do more for us than God.

When Israel was attacked, a few people survived to warn others of the grave consequences of their sin. Perhaps that history lesson can serve as a warning for us to not place our confidence in whatever panic tells us. Spending time in stillness before the Lord is the shepherd's crook around our waist that gently leads us back to the pathway of his purpose. May we habitually depend on God because we regularly meet with him in the quiet.

~ Belong Blessing ~

When you sense a time has come in your life for you to stop, be still, and listen to the Lord's voice, may your desire and schedule make a way for that to happen. And as you take that time to listen, may the panic monsters not jump into the middle of your emotions, stirring you up in all the wrong ways. May you remember the only choice you have to make in the moment is to listen for which direction the Lord intends your own back road to go. And as you begin to travel that way, may your chief inclination be to pray more and panic less because you've met with him.

Ten

Looking into Your People

Don't chase people who do not value you; link arms with those
who do and do great things, together.

Lisa Whittle

INSTEAD OF FEELING on the outside of both virtual and real-life
gatherings, those of us struggling to belong need to look in places
that perpetually quench our thirst for a sense of belonging, like in
God's Word and in the quiet.

Another place God wants us to look is in our present relationships.

To know our belonging place, we can first ask and answer these
questions for ourselves:

Am I taking for granted or even ignoring relationships I have
   that God has placed in my life today?

Am I too busy looking at other friendships through the lens
   of social media or at the neighboring table, wishing I was in
   their circle instead of appreciating my own?

Do I have a hospitable spirit for the people near me?

At the most basic level, my people are the four residing with me under my roof. Or at least, the four who originally resided under my roof. My twin sons graduated high school recently, which is something else because they just graduated from kindergarten last year. That's the funny thing about time: we can look in the rearview mirror and see it moved miles in a moment. In reality, we've lived over 9,467,085 minutes within their eighteen years. Within those minutes we've had heartache happen and dreams get realized. We've lived a mixed bag of good and difficult and hard and easy moments of side-splitting laughter, heart-splitting tears, and heart-healing love. We've traveled road after road of life together, and I will always belong with whom I affectionately term my "favorite four"—even if our belonging together changes as the kids grow up.

At the risk of sounding like an awful wife and mama, let me tell you there was a time when, as I considered my place and my people, I failed to count those who share my address. Now, I know God desires us all to have a larger belonging place within friendships and community. We'll talk more about that in future chapters, don't you fret. But it's important we don't gloss right over several valuable places and people with whom we already belong.

This might sound a little ding-a-ling, but go with me here: if I hand you a piece of paper and ask you to roll it into a cone and point it toward your definite *in* place, what would you see when you looked through it? Where are you *in* right now? You're in somewhere, even if it's just sitting in the back pew at church. Or in the living room of your own home. Or in the congested carpool line or on the predictable suburban sidewalks or in an artsy downtown apartment. It may not seem like much, but it's the location to accept as your starting place of belonging.

Narrow your focus, dear one, and expand your sense of belonging. Create a kind of holy tunnel vision and let your starting place and people sharpen into view.

There've been times in my life when, if you would have said this to me, I would have replied, "Listen, I've sat in the back pew and at the corner table before, and just being in the building doesn't mean I belong." I get that, I really do. Depending on circumstances, even the family living room can seem more like hostile territory than a haven of happiness. Nonetheless, those spaces *are* launching places for expanding our sense of belonging. The hard part is, after we recognize our launching places, we sometimes have to wait to be able to feel like we belong there.

But we do not wait helplessly. We wait expectantly.

I read recently about a comet hunter who admitted to logging nine hundred hours at an eyepiece before he saw his first comet.[1] And his advice to other comet hunters goes like this:

1. Stay at the eyepiece and keep looking.
2. Watch the sky every day.
3. Study as many established comets as you can so you'll recognize one when it appears.
4. Be patient. The do-or-die approach rarely works.

When I think of this in terms of finding our place and people, it seems like a good parallel plan.

1. Stay at your launching place and keep looking.
2. Watch your own life and begin noticing where you already belong.
3. Study ways you can reach out to others so you can recognize a good opportunity to do so.
4. Be patient, because larger belonging places are rarely forged overnight.

The Lord never acts in arbitrary ways. He acts in purposeful ways.

And the LORD set a time, saying, "Tomorrow the LORD will do this thing in the land. And the next day the LORD did this thing." (Exod. 9:5–6)

Every comet that shows itself to us is on the divine calendar. The end of every struggle is on the divine calendar too—including our struggle to belong as we're meant to belong. We need only remain at the eyepiece (or the living room or sidewalk or Starbucks patio or city park) to see it. But as we wait, let's not miss his showering splendor.

I imagine that while those hunting for comets sit and wait, they see all kinds of other marvelous finds. Fast-rotating satellites. Quick-draw shooting stars. Ancient-named constellations. A thousand pictures of God's wonder made visible while staring through the eyepiece.

It makes me ask myself, *As you wait for your own larger belonging place to show, Kristen, what other pictures of beauty can you find where you are right now?*

This lesson was brought home especially well after I returned from summer vacation with my family. Having largely ignored social media in favor of family shenanigans at one of our favorite out-of-town spots, I plopped down on our porch and visited the ol' Instagram and Facebook. And within about two minutes of social media grazing, I gobbled down one big, disappointing fact: several friends were getting together without me.

On the one hand, some of those friends had invited me to join them. I wasn't able to do so on account of conflicting vacation plans. No big thing. But on the other hand, other friends were also getting together and hadn't asked me to join them in the first place. Of course, they had no obligation to ask. They're in charge of who they hang out with and when. Yet here they were on my Instagram feed, bossing all those "on the outside" feelings I didn't know were there till I opened the Insta-door and let them in.

I'm on to them, however. This isn't my first rodeo with FOMO (fear of missing out). No, ma'am. I've wrestled that steer to the ground, and on that day, I was in no mood to go backward.

For me, in that moment, I sensed the Lord asking me to name all the places I belonged, right then and there. So I opened the "notes" app on my phone and began to make a new old-fashioned list. I typed "Where I Belong" and listed the following:

God's daughter, Jesus's beloved

wife to David

mama to James, Ethan, and Faith

daughter, sister, aunt, niece, and cousin of the O'Neill and
Meeks families

daughter-in-law, aunt, and sister-in-law in the Strong family

friend to Aimée, Alli, Cheryl, Rebecca, Connie, Kim, Holley,
Lisa-Jo, Salena, and others

member of my church, Village Seven

member of Cornerstone Community

Black Forest resident in Colorado Springs

military wife and encourager

writer to women from my own space and for the (in)courage
community

frequent patron at Barnes & Noble and the R&R Café, where
some of the staff know me by name

Then I sat back in my chair and looked that list over. Honestly, it was longer than I thought it would be, and it was a deeply meaningful list. It put a muzzle on those bossy, I-don't-belong feelings with tangible proof that indeed, I *did* belong. It was just the holy tunnel vision I needed: my own eyepiece showing me where I already belonged instead of all the places I didn't.

And since that time, I've referred to that list again and again—as well as added to it—whenever I start to believe, once again, that I don't belong. As a friend told me recently, sometimes the problem is we simply discount those places we do belong and then compensate for this by trying to belong in more places than we've been designed to.

If you struggle with those same bossy feelings, perhaps you'll want to make your own list electronically. Or you may want to use a page in your journal or on the back of your last grocery receipt. You can name your people and places out loud, but it's helpful to see them in black-and-white too. When you start to doubt your belonging, narrow your vision to include your people with whom you belong today. It's a way of saying, *You're always good, Lord, and today, this is enough.*

See in letters and words all the ways God is providing you with a place—even if the belonging is not to the degree you may like.

And once you name those places, belong to them like there's no tomorrow. Belong where you're supposed to belong most. Pour into your top priority people in this particular season. Doing so will affirm not only your belonging places but those of your already-people too.

No one person is meant to be on the inside of every circle. But everyone *is* on the inside somewhere. We need only to first look where that place is rather than where we wish it were. When this happens, we can discover that our back road to belonging is lined with people who love us and support us right now.

We need only to narrow our focus to expand our sense of belonging.

I got a firsthand chance in narrowing my focus only yesterday. As I tapped out this chapter, we received word our beloved son, who had wanted to attend his dream military school since fifth grade and was accepted into that school this spring, will be medically released on account of several injuries he received during basic training. When he originally called to tell us this may be happening, he said some of the most heartbreaking words to his dad and me: "Dad and Mama, I sure hope you're not too disappointed in me for having to leave."

Oh, how some words can cut through the tender flesh of the mama heart.

After assuring him there was no way, no how we could be disappointed in him for this, we told him we loved him because of who he is in Christ and because he is our child, not because of what he does or where he gets his education. We told him that, as long as he's okay, we would all be okay with whatever direction the Lord sent him. We told him that when he out-processed, we'd be waiting at home with the widest arms to welcome him in as he figures out what and where his next steps will be.

And when that precious, long 'n' lanky boy landed on our doorstep, we all but hugged his neck clean off. We did our best to make the safest possible place for that beloved kid to figure out his larger belonging place. We hunkered down and huddled in right around him and yet gave him room to expand as he, in that safe place, leaned in to Christ, his forever belonging place.

It occurred to me this is what Jesus does for us. As we narrow our focus and lean in to Jesus and our close-by people, we find then that we're best set up to lean in to our larger belonging place. We have the security of a foundation to belonging, so we're ready to enlarge it and find those other places we want to belong as well. We have a sturdy space from which to build upon, learn from, and reach out toward others.

Sometimes the most unexpected paths turn out to be the most obvious roads to our belonging place.

Yes, stay at the eyepiece and keep looking.

And keep finding.

traveling companion: MICHELLE

There was a time in Michelle's life when she enjoyed knee-deep participation in social media as a way to stay connected to friends and family and "up-to-date" with its latest and greatest buffet of offerings. It also allowed her to share what the Lord was doing in her life.[2] At one point, however, she realized social media was sabotaging her own sense of belonging. As she spent extended time perusing Facebook posts and pictures, she found herself comparing her body to other women's bodies and her social calendar to other friends' calendars. She became angry when she wasn't invited to friends' get-togethers and frustrated over comments people did or didn't leave to her own posts. Michelle began to realize that through social media, she had placed her self-worth and sense of belonging in other people's hands, not the hands of the One who created her.

As Michelle continued to allow herself to be torn down by what she saw on her screen, she sensed the Lord lifting her up. In her heart, she could feel him saying, *Spend more time with me. I want to tell you how beautiful you are. I want to fill your heart, mind, and soul. I want to give you all the desires of your heart.* He wanted more of her time to bring her to her most meaningful belonging place.

In order to do that, however, Michelle decided she needed to make a major change to her online life. In her own way of employing holy tunnel vision, she deleted her Facebook account. This opened up a space for her to focus on the relationships in her life that mattered most: her relationships with the Lord, her husband, and her close family and friends.

As Michelle and her husband's family grew, she saw a shift in how she felt about her belonging place. She stopped investing time in social media's letdowns and disappointments and started investing in joy and satisfaction found in her real-life relationships. She lost contact with some friends, yes. But as she focused on the Lord and the relationships closest to her, she realized life can be sweeter when you desire less.

Since Michelle lives several states away from family and many friends, she still enjoys using Instagram as a way of staying connected to them. However, she keeps the settings on private and maintains a tight rein on who gets access to her account. If she gets an invite from someone she desires to encourage or who encourages her, she accepts. If she gets an invite from someone else, she declines. It's her way of protecting her heart and mind as she intentionally focuses on what and who matter most in her life.

Michelle makes it clear that because her strict social media policy is right for her, that doesn't mean it's right for others. The Holy Spirit speaks to us all individually. But for Michelle, this move has been vital for helping her curate a real belonging place by cutting down unnecessary distractions to her life and teardowns to her heart. It has been her way of staying at the eyepiece so she invests in real-life relationships and knows real-life belonging.

~Belong Blessing~

When you're frustrated because your belonging place looks different than you want it to, may you not assume you're the one person who won't ever feel and know you belong. When those "on the outside" feelings threaten to rise up and throw you toward despair, may God move them far, far away from you as he ushers in a fresh wave of peace. May you stay at your own eyepiece and appreciate where you belong at this moment. And when you struggle to see your place and people, may the Lord narrow your focus on them as your own launching pad to an expanded belonging place.

eleven

Growing Up and Out

Simple steps can change the way we do community with those who live in closest proximity to us. Little decisions can reveal the great needs waiting out there, crying to be met, as we open our literal door. To befriend. To be a light in the darkness.

Jen Schmidt, *Just Open the Door*

A QUIET BACK ROAD REQUIRES the patience and eyes-wide-open vision that allow us to see the stunning views of God's provision for each of us. But it also provides a suitable place for us to consider where he wants us to expand our circle and sense of belonging.

After we spend time caring for our heart's soil by looking in God's Word, in God's presence, and in our priority relationships, we are better able to grow up and out toward our larger belonging place because we're better rooted in Christ. We can move forward from the place of already-abundance God gives rather than from perceived slim pickings. "They feast on the abundance of your house, and you give them drink from the river of your delights" (Ps. 36:8). Yes, please, to owning that this is meant for me. And you. When we align ourselves with God's truth *in* us, we'll find the pathway illuminated toward God's truth *for* us. And then we can walk that path toward welcoming others into our life as well.

When I was growing up in Oklahoma, every one of my neighbors shared my last name—they were literally family. I went to college only an hour away, alongside several family members and friends. Until I married my husband, a newly coined officer in the US Air Force, I never had to work to make friends. I always had my place and people.

When our newlywed selves moved from Oklahoma to Ohio, I had little desire to initiate conversations with people I didn't know. In some ways, I didn't even know how to do that. Still, I behaved in a self-defeating way because I didn't want to do the work of putting myself out there in different environments. I often didn't accept invitations from others, and if I did I would come home disappointed because I didn't really connect with anyone. At the same time, I wasn't *trying* to connect with anyone.

When I mull over this conduct, I shake my head at my own shoot-myself-in-the-foot attitude. But research shows this is normal human behavior. For those of us who want to expand our sense of belonging within a community, most assume that means we have the desire to build those necessary relationships that lead to belonging. People who are lonely feel more negative, more critical, and more judgmental than those who aren't lonely.[1] Similarly, those of us struggling to fit in may lean toward actions that work against us and our real need to belong.

It turns out "being acutely lonely is as stressful as being punched in the face by a stranger—and massively increases your risk of depression. . . . The only real way out of our epidemic of despair is for all of us, together, to begin to meet those human needs—for deep connection, to the things that really matter in life."[2] Since one of our most basic psychological needs is to feel we belong, it's imperative we put the smackdown on our inner saboteur by growing up and out toward others.

Research further states that one thing that fights loneliness (as well as other unmet psychological needs) is giving people autonomy and control over their work.[3] It's a positive step for our mental and physical health to give ourselves the power of big decisions that ensure a degree of movement toward our larger place of belonging. We can say no to working against ourselves and yes to God showing us how to take the reins on getting ourselves going in a positive direction.

More or less, this is what I believe the Lord wanted me to know in those early years of my marriage. Since friends weren't going to fall from the sky and into my lap, I needed to stop opening the door expecting someone to be there unless I'd invited them to be there. The only way to guarantee never finding a group of folks to connect with was to never try again.

So, yeah, it's important to know where to look for people with whom we enjoy a sense of belonging. It's even more important to take that hard first step toward them. While this requires a little initiative, it carries with it the hopeful message that there's always room at the table God picks out for each of us.

However, we have to be willing to stand up and walk over to that table first. And great day, can that ever make you shake in your boots. Fighting the isolation and loneliness and awkwardness and extending that invitation is just plain hard. It's scary to stand in the windy, exposed chasm between you and the other person. I know. But it's also worth it. The apostle Paul wrote, "Therefore welcome one another as Christ has welcomed you, for the glory of God" (Rom. 15:7). It's for our own good and God's glory to stand up and clip-clop right over to that table.

First John 4:19 states, short and sweet, why we should go first: "We love because he first loved us." Jesus, motivated by his love for us, went first by sacrificing his life on the cross so we could have abundant life in Christ. Therefore, we can go first and love others from the overflow of Christ.

After we've identified and put the kibosh on any self-sabotaging actions we may be doing that work against us, we can take the first difficult steps to get going in the right direction. It helps, I believe, to think of this in terms of small. You don't need a big ol' posse to belong to; you just need a few people who offer you a larger sense of place. Between you and me, I get weary of the word *community* altogether. Not always, mind you, just when it carries a connotation of I-must-have-several-besties-or-I'm-doing-it-wrong. Or I need enough people to fill a town. It implies *I can't belong without big numbers of people in my circles.* And I don't think that's true. In Jesus's day-to-day ministry life, he hung with a dozen people. He spoke to and moved in the lives of thousands, yes, because he made himself available to many. But his inner circle contained twelve disciples, and within that was an even tighter circle of three.

To a certain degree, belonging is about truly being where we already are. It's making ourselves available for God to bring us where he wants to bring us and toward those he wants to welcome into our lives. We can take one small step to move in the direction of those around us: our fellow neighbors, coworkers, churchgoers, dog walkers, ballplayers, schoolteachers, classroom helpers, parents, and others we see as we move throughout our day. We can't make ourselves available to every person we pass by through life, of course. But when we combine a willingness to be available with those whom God asks us to be available for, we're on the right back road to belonging.

When God moves your heart toward another, simply do what you can to be a light to that person. It's the little things that are the big, important things. Maybe you offer to take her chicken noodle soup because she has a terrible cold. Maybe you offer to pick her kids up from school or get her a cup of coffee from your kitchen or the drive-thru. You can invite her into your home, of course, but you can do something smaller too. Maybe it's as simple as asking how she's doing and actually listening to the answer. Maybe it's as easy as smiling at her and telling her you like her cute shoes. Those small acts have the potential to become building blocks to a friendship that might move you toward your stronger belonging place.

I know it's hard to take those first steps to get going in the right direction, but there's something that's harder to do still, harder to accept. At some point, you're going to extend your hand in friendship and it won't be taken as quickly as you hoped. Or maybe not at all. Here's the good news, however: because you looked around to those folks already in your life, listened for God's direction as to whom to make yourself specifically available, *and* followed through with action, you did what you were supposed to do. You obeyed and followed where God led. You're not responsible for what happens after that. Outcomes are up to him. Release those outcomes and the effort you put into them.

• • •

When we expend effort on others that we hope will produce fruit, sometimes it flat-out won't. Sometimes God has a different kind of fruit in mind, away from the obvious. He may want to grow something inside us through our "follow-through," for example. No matter the results, we may have to crawl out to the edge of the limb. Whether something substantial dangles off the branch is up to the Lord. Sometimes God wants us to be a simple road stop blessing in someone's day rather than a regular destination. We will save ourselves a lot of anxiety if we, in the words of the great theologian Carrie Underwood, let Jesus take the wheel on the specifics.

With subsequent military transfers, I became pretty comfortable "making the first move" in friendship with someone. In a baptism-by-fire kind of way, I became unafraid to talk to people I didn't know. I'm adept at asking questions and breezing over small talk easily but not awkwardly. But in spite of all this, sometimes I *still* find myself alone in a crowd, and I can't help but think it would be lovely—really lovely—if I didn't have to make the first move. It would be fresh-air-fabulous if just one person would do the work of seeking me out first so connecting would feel less like a chore.

But I realize this as well: if it's easy for me to do all the "right" things yet still struggle with insecurity or uneasiness around others, how often do others—especially those who find approaching people and striking up a conversation difficult—feel the same way?

There's just no way to get around it: making friends is hard. Expanding our belonging place is hard. It takes purpose and effort. It takes work. Quite often it takes more time than I'd like.

There's also no way to get around this: it's always worth it to keep working at it. Reading through Scripture one day, I was struck afresh with a new angle to an old proverb:

> Go to the ant, O sluggard;
> consider her ways, and be wise.
> Without having any chief,
> officer, or ruler,
> she prepares her bread in summer
> and gathers her food in harvest. (Prov. 6:6–8)

While I usually associate the wisdom and warnings of Proverbs such as this one to apply to one's willingness to work and provide, I read it here as referring to putting hard work into developing friendships and building a belonging place. If we put in the time and effort God asks, we will one day gather our own harvest of life-giving, spirit-building, heart-helping friendships.

What a beautiful place to grow up and out.

traveling companion:
EMMY

Emmy, a wife and mama to two children, enjoyed a longtime, close relationship with a couple of friends when all their spouses worked together. They were family as much as friends, and their kids were raised together. But as is the way with jobs and life, the friends' spouses were eventually transferred to different company divisions, so they moved away from one another. But after several years of living in different corners of the country, Emmy and her two friends discovered their families would be moving to the same location one last time. Emmy couldn't wait to dive deep into their friendship once again.

However, after everyone relocated to the same town, things did not go as Emmy expected. For a year she tried to orchestrate coffees, dinners, and general "hang out time" with them and their families, but almost every offer met excuses and rejection. The more she reached out, the more she began to see she was the only one reaching out. This hurt her feelings more than once.

Emmy and her friends would still get coffee sometimes, but when they did, it felt rushed and competitive. As a result, Emmy walked away from those short get-togethers more defeated than rejuvenated. Eventually, she realized she couldn't make this friendship something it wasn't.

While Emmy had to go through the grieving process brought on by a removed sense of belonging, she also realized where she belonged in one season may not be where she belonged in another. She couldn't deny their friendship had changed, though not by her choice. She couldn't expend most of the effort and expect the fruit to look a certain way. Now, while she still gets angry and sad about it sometimes, she accepts there must be room for letting go within her belonging place.

More importantly, Emmy realized she had ignored other relationships God had placed in her life as she tried to force her relationship with these two friends to resemble what it once had. When she released these friends from her life, she had the room to see and invest in God's provision of new ones.

Because of this, she enjoyed a renewed sense of belonging with her family. She joined a Bunco group and discovered she came alive when mentoring new homeschooling moms. A short while later, God blessed her with a couple of friends with whom she enjoys a back-and-forth level of friendship to a degree she'd never experienced before.

Yes, for a time Emmy's friendship view did not look as she hoped. However, she looked around at the folks already in her life, listened for God's direction as to whom to make herself available, and followed through with action. With time and patience, she found exactly what she hoped to find: the makings of a beautiful belonging place.[4]

~Belong Blessing~

When you feel paralyzed from loneliness and heavyhearted from isolation, may the Lord help you take just one small step toward others. May he move your heart not to feel overwhelmed from that one small thing but excited and willing to be available to whom God asks you to be available. May your efforts to go first in friendship lead to a deeper sense of belonging. But if they don't, may you have peace in knowing that, with time, your follow-through will bring about good, good things from the Lord.

twelve

Talking More, Listening Less

I just began to tell myself the good news of Jesus over and over, and it began to stick. When I caught myself listening to or repeating bad news to myself, I immediately countered with what I knew to be true. . . . So, "I can't do this" becomes "I can't do this *without You*."

Hayley Morgan, *Preach to Yourself*

ONE OF MY FAVORITE WRITERS, artists, and Instagram follows is Ruth Chou Simons, aka @gracelaced, a creative whose wielding of paintbrush and pen result in wondrous beauty and astounding hope. I'm convinced this wife and mama to six (!!!) boys is positively anointed with talent, and her creativity is a mighty tool of encouragement in my life and the lives of many others. Her artwork goes beyond decoratory house stuff to reflect the Word alive and the way it works into our hearts. In Ruth's words, the Word of God does heart surgery on her.[1] Out of that comes her own "preaching truth to my own heart" posts (#preachingtruthtomyownheart), in which she shares soul-satisfying Scripture like this:

> For all the places we go today, Lord, lead us back to You. For all the ways we can fly today, Lord, help us find refuge beneath Your wings. For all that will glitter and dazzle us today, Lord, fix our eyes on You. For all that vies for our allegiance today, Lord, remind us that we belong to You. And for all that we must do this day, Lord, fill us FIRST with Your Word, Amen.
>
> It's not too late to set aside what's pressing and set the Lord before you (Ps. 16:8), and trust Him for your day. His mercies are new every morning (Lam. 3:22–23).[2]

Ruth is one I read because her words reflect the Word alive to me. She preaches truth to my own heart. I believe the Lord uses her as a tool to share his faithful, foundational truth in a fresh way. What's more, I often recite her wise words out loud. I do that because heaven knows I do a lot of reciting of ugly stuff too, stuff planted and repeated by Satan himself. His native language is lies (John 8:44), and even though I know this, he's pretty apt at making me question my worth and belonging place in this world.

• • •

Before the US Air Force moved us to the sunshine-swaddled town of Colorado Springs, our family was stationed in Hawaii. (I know, I know, we do hard things for our country!) During our time there, we island-hopped on several occasions to see more of our country's beautiful fiftieth state. While at the airport before a trip, something happened that will go down as one of the oddest things I've ever experienced, something that gave me a very real picture of the garbage-spewing Satan does to steer us off track.

After going through security and making the usual bathroom stop, my three young kids and I stopped into a small travel store for bottled waters. Meanwhile, David headed down to our departure gate, where he finished a phone call for work. I grabbed a *People* magazine for myself and ushered the kids over to the checkout line. Focused on getting to our gate in time, the kids and I didn't share much conversation beyond how much time was left before we boarded our flight.

When it was my turn to pay, the person working the register took my cash and then stared at me through narrowed, piercing eyes. As he stood there, casually holding my money, he proceeded to berate me something fierce. Right there, in front of my kids and fellow travelers, he told me I was a terrible mother and that my kids would grow up and want nothing to do with me. He told me I was a disgusting person who would be disliked by everyone. He said all this while waving my cash midair, dark eyes trained on my wide-eyed self. He said it loud enough for others to hear, certainly, but in an even, direct voice. It was as if he was placing the most ordinary order at a coffee shop rather than gushing ugliness.

For several seconds, I just stared, awash in disbelief. Finally, I snapped out of it, interrupted his calm yet upsetting diatribe, and said, "Sir, I just want to pay for my stuff here. Finish my transaction *right now*."

He glared at me a few seconds longer, then finally handed me my change. My heart thumped in my chest, and I just wanted to do an about-face and go. I hadn't done anything wrong, I knew, but I was as embarrassed as all get-out. My kids and I grabbed our goods and turned to leave, and a woman behind me tapped my arm and said, "Ma'am, I've never in my life witnessed something like that, and I applaud you for your gracious response. That was crazy!" She shook her head back and forth.

I smiled and told her thank you. Really, I was just so shocked I hadn't consciously chosen my response. I just wanted to get us the heck out of Dodge.

Hawaii may be paradise, but in that moment, it felt more like a stripped-down barren island. Sometimes you simply need to get to friendlier territory fast.

We walked to our gate, me fielding questions from the kids. "Mama, why was that man talking like that?" "Why was he so mean?"

I told them I didn't know, but that it's a good thing we listen to what Jesus says about us more than other people.

Here's the thing about that encounter: in a nutshell, that man, whom I'd never met, said my deepest inside fears out loud. Relationships are my chief currency, so the thought of losing key relationships breaks my heart into a thousand pieces. It attacks the very center of my belonging place here on earth. I could sell millions of books and win all the literary awards, and it would be meaningless if my kids wanted nothing to do with me. I know that travel store encounter was over-the-top and, really, just plain insane. Still, it unnerved me. It was as if the devil himself said the words rather than this stranger.

We talked in an earlier chapter about how, when the enemy threatens your belonging place, leaning into God's Word gets him to back off. We talked about how the enemy will pick at our flaws and blow them out of proportion, yes. But he'll also attack the essence of who we are and what we do. He will gladly and enthusiastically stir up our worst fears, and before long our actions stem from his lies rather than God's truth. We abandon our own back road altogether by acting like we don't belong, even though that isn't so.

Often, he'll start in on us when we're in the middle of something ordinary, like buying water for a plane ride. Or when we're standing there doing any number of everyday things in our regular way, like sorting laundry or making a dinner plan. Out of nowhere, this voice comes.

You're a terrible mother.
You're too slow and stupid to get this right.
You'll never belong there, because they don't want you.
You don't deserve to belong here or anywhere.

The voice probably doesn't shout but speaks calmly, smoothly. Even as you and I do our part to look in the right places to belong, a lot of us still fight a narrative in our own head that tries to tell us it

123

won't happen. That narrative may come from words spoken out loud by other people or spoken silently by our own inner critic, introduced and repeated by our insidious enemy. Whatever the case, the words spoken to us become the truth we believe about ourselves. And while it's generally a good idea to listen more than talk when conversing with others, I believe those struggling to belong need to talk more than listen when talking to ourselves. We need to rehearse the good stuff that springs from a place of beauty, not vicious lies.

Numerous studies show that speaking what we want to learn out loud helps us remember it.[3] If this is true, it stands to reason that speaking the truth about *ourselves* out loud helps us remember that truth too. As it often does, research echoes what the Bible said long ago.

> I will also speak of your testimonies before kings
> and shall not be put to shame. (Ps. 119:46)

When we speak the truth of what God says about us and has done for us, whether before others or before our own tired selves, we will not be put to shame. We will not be shoulder-hunched. As we travel our own back road to belonging, we will not be stuck in our own *I'm-a-loser* loop.

We can voice the truth of God's desire to get us to the other side of what we're going through.

We can speak aloud our gratitude for what we have.

Each of us can say, "I am enough," and not stop there. Each of us can also say, "This is enough. Where I am and what I have is enough. I am thankful for what I have and who I have and where I am today, and I will lean into this instead of languishing over what I wish I had or where I wish I was."

• • •

Speaking truth out loud is one big way I rehearse beauty. Our purpose of belonging is to know Jesus more and to move closer to who God created us to be, and he created us for his good purposes. At the end of this book are several Scripture passages that specifically speak to God's desire for us to know we belong. The Bible is the most important place for us to get truth, and when we make an effort to take it in we can then speak its truths out loud. If you're sitting next to me anytime I work on a writing project, you'll hear me saying, "For God has not given [me] a spirit of fear, but of power and of love and of a sound mind" (2 Tim. 1:7 NKJV). Writing is a job I love, but it's scary too. I need to converse with the Lord about that and let his Word remind me that I have what it takes to do what he asks.

Others help me rehearse beauty too. Charles Spurgeon said it well as to why it's good to read others' responses to gospel truth:

> "As they go through the Valley of Baca they make it a place of springs; the early rain also covers it with pools." Psalm 84:6
>
> This teaches us that the comfort obtained by one may prove helpful to another, just as the springs would be enjoyed by the company who came after. When we read some book that is really helpful and encouraging, we recognize that the author has gone ahead of us and discovered these refreshing springs for us as well as for himself. Many books have been like wells drilled by a pilgrim for himself but have proved quite as useful to others.[4]

There are books and resources, like Ruth's Instagram page, that have been wells the authors drilled for themselves but have provided a cool drink of water for me. When I read them, I rehearse truth. When I speak them out loud to myself, they take me one step closer to paradise and away from the desert—regardless of my circumstances. They help me receive truth and rehearse the good stuff by relaying God's heart to my own.

So when you feel that your belonging place is threatened or that you just may be the exception to finding one, go ahead and talk more than you listen. Get up in the morning and say out loud what is true, even if you don't yet feel it. Move through your afternoon with God's assurances on your lips. Welcome your evening with his promises directed toward your own heart.

Get to friendlier territory fast. Talk to yourself about how you do belong more than you listen to yourself about how you don't. Rehearse beauty and truth, not ugly garbage.

Then repeat.

traveling companion:
HAGAR

One thing I love about the Bible? Some stories are so blow-your-mind crazy you'd think they were made up. Nope. They're as true as can be. The story of Abram and Sarai, later known as Abraham and Sarah, is one such example.

As told in Genesis 16, Abram and Sarai were a couple "getting on in years" with no children. Because Sarai had not been able to conceive a child, she gave Hagar, her servant, to her husband as another wife. At the risk of stating the obvious, yes, this is a horrible, terrible, no good idea. Just the thought of it would make most of us don our best Julia Sugarbaker voice and ask, "Have you just *completely* lost your mind?!" How could Sarai not just allow but encourage such a thing?

Well, in those days, this arrangement was not an uncommon occurrence.

First of all, desperation can make an otherwise lucid person do outrageous things. . . . Secondly, the custom of acquiring an heir through a maidservant was practiced in parts of the ancient world.

The New International Commentary quotes four ancient texts that suggest practices similar to the one Sarai offered to Abram. "An Old Assyrian marriage contract" included this instruction, "If within two years she has not procured offspring for him, only she may buy a maid-servant and even later on, after she procures somehow an infant for him, she may sell her wherever she pleases."[5]

It's imperative to mention that while this was the cultural practice at the time, it doesn't mean God supported it. Here, he certainly didn't. He doesn't support injustice. People are unjust to one another, but God isn't.

When Hagar did conceive a child, she began to treat Sarai poorly. When Sarai returned the favor by treating her harshly as well, Hagar got herself out of Dodge.

Here's what happened next.

> The angel of the LORD found her by a spring of water in the wilderness, the spring on the way to Shur. And he said, "Hagar, servant of Sarai, where have you come from and where are you going?" She said, "I am fleeing from my mistress Sarai." The angel of the LORD said to her, "Return to your mistress and submit to her." The angel of the LORD also said to her, "I will surely multiply your offspring so that they cannot be numbered for multitude." (Gen. 16:7–10)

Some Bible scholars believe the angel of the Lord who found Hagar may have been God himself. Either way, I love that he asked Hagar specific questions that directly related to her sense of belonging. Did the Lord or his angel already know the answer to where she'd come from and where she was headed? Absolutely. But he wanted to encourage her to speak it out loud. He wanted her to know he could be trusted as her confidant.

Then, Scripture says, the angel spoke encouragement to Hagar, including the directive that her belonging place was with Abram and Sarai. Amid circumstances that seemed impossibly difficult, he would make a way for her there through her offspring.

In response, Hagar spoke these words, "You are a God of seeing. . . . Truly here I have seen him who looks after me" (v. 13). It's interesting to note here that Hagar gave God the name *El Roi*, meaning "a God of seeing." No other Old Testament character names him like this, only this Egyptian maidservant whose circumstances were dreadfully un-ideal.[6] She spoke God's truth out loud: "He sees me." And, as a result, she was encouraged in her own belonging place.

~Belong Blessing~

May God's voice be the loudest voice you hear, dear one. When the enemy tries to shame you, condemn you, hurt you, or isolate you, may you stop, look to truth, and listen to your own voice repeating it out loud. May you be receptive to letting others who've gone ahead of you speak good things into your life too. May your shoulders sit relaxed and your posture at ease because you know God sees you. And may you know that because he sees you, he knows where you best belong. He will faithfully see you there.

thirteen

Helping the Hard (but Worth It) Way

> The biggest kind of self-deception is for us to think we've got our lives under control. We're all just one stomach bug, one bad report card, one month of missed work, one negative interview, one lost wallet away from losing all the bits and pieces of our lives we hold on to with such tight fists.
>
> Lisa-Jo Baker, *Never Unfriended*

As WE WORK TO SPEAK TRUTH out loud about ourselves, we also must speak truth out loud to others. That is, if we feel we have "our people" around us yet lack a sense of belonging with them, we may need to elevate the degree of what we share with one or more loved ones.

It's a kind of self-deception to believe we're all we need to belong. It's a myth to think that if we just prop ourselves up enough to look like we've got our act together all the time, if the house is clean enough, if our kids are setting the curve in every class at school, and if we're not struggling with one of the top ten sins, then we're all good to belong where we're supposed to.

You know what? We might be able to achieve that for a minute or two. Eventually, however, we're going to run into our limitations, into things outside our control. One of those spinning plates—if not the whole kit and caboodle—is going to crash onto the concrete floor.

And it's a different kind of self-deception to believe that if we tamp down any and all vulnerability that belonging requires, it will not come out in other, less desirable ways. It *will* come out.

When we moved every threeish years, two of my kids dealt with the transition by processing their feelings out loud. "Why do we have to move again?" "Why can't Daddy just work from here like he's been doing? Didn't they like the work he did?" I fielded all the questions and we hashed stuff out, often the same concerns over and over again. My third kiddo, however, handled the change in our place and people differently. Basically, he dealt with it by spitting vinegar at the other four of us. He remained closed up about his thoughts and feelings about moving, but he'd go the extra mile or ten to pick a fight with his siblings. He'd walk a microscopically fine line with his dad and me. He'd outright refuse to be "bossed" by us any more than he thought necessary.

With experience, we came to expect the behavior, and of course we offered extra grace for a while. Just because our kids were forced to leave their belonging place because of Dad's job didn't mean they had to like it. We gave them the time they needed to accept it, and they each did so on their own timeline. Not surprisingly, it took the kiddo who refused to talk about it longer to accept each move. Eventually, though, after we gave him the space to share in his own way about what was going on inside, he would open up. Not a great deal, but enough to release some of his tension.

Having a strong sense of belonging and showing vulnerability are both contributing factors to positive mental health. One secular study by Stanford psychologist Gregory Walton found that when people shared their stories and experiences about the difficulties in their lives with others, they were able to lessen their association of bad days with not belonging. Professor Walton states, "We often operate from very biased information. We have our own experience and can only see others from the outside. Many of us are having the same difficulties, but no one is showing it, and so we can feel isolated and depressed."[1]

Sharing how we're doing with the difficulties in our life—marriage concerns, parenting matters, unfulfilling job issues, or other troubles—helps create the sense of belonging we want and need. Reflecting or sharing about our struggles takes all those inside thoughts from that subjective, *something must be wrong with me* part of our swirling minds and makes them stand outside in the clearer light of day. It allows ourselves and others to see that we're not so unique in our circumstances. Others have been there too, so we *do* belong.

Brené Brown writes that true belonging only happens when we present our authentic, imperfect selves to the world.[2] So, if we want to truly belong, we need to get real about how we're really doing. Perhaps this is why Proverbs 18:1 warns, "Whoever isolates himself seeks his own desire; he breaks out against all sound judgment." Perpetual isolation leads to desolation of the spirit. Desolation of the spirit leads us away from sound judgment, something that messes with our inside thought life as we seek to know and find our place of belonging.

Two words that are the deadbolts on the door of isolation? *I'm fine.*

You know how it goes. You're having a hard time with your friend's cold shoulder or your husband's late work hours or the sudden raise in rent or your kid's refusal to take school seriously. Your bills go up at the same time you get a cut in salary. Or something good happens, like you earn that job promotion or other new opportunity. But when the lights go out, your fears light up and you think to yourself, *They've made a terrible mistake, and they're going to be so disappointed in me when they discover I don't belong there.*

But when people ask how you're doing, you tell them you're A-OK, all is fine.

Really, however, you feel a segment of your security slipping—or what you thought was security—in your sense of belonging, and those old panic monsters double down their efforts to rile up your insides. Not to mention it takes real work to share your struggles. It takes work, time, and *vulnerability*. Who wants to put others out when they have their own, much bigger things going on? That's what I tell myself, anyway. *Why would I burden others with my burdens? Who do I think I am, anyway?*

I love what author Lisa-Jo Baker says about *I'm fine*, words that shut down dialogue before it starts:

> Fine is so dangerous, isn't it? Fine means the end of a conversation. The beginning of nothing. If Truth can set us free, best to start living in those places, right? It's hard to admit our un-fine moments. But I've always found it's in those moments that people can actually GET to us to help us. We need people. We are a body. And if one part is all bashed up and bleeding it hurts everywhere else.[3]

When we want to deepen our sense of belonging, showing our vulnerability allows others to get to us. Once we unlock that door and let another tend to us, like the friends who lowered the sick man on a mat through a roof to Jesus, we are strengthened because of their faith (Luke 5:17–39). We internalize the truth that Jesus's burden is feather-light as we see his teaching fulfilled through those kind, listening loved ones.

Of course, if you're asked how you're doing and you really are fine, you can say that if it's true. You can also say it if you're, for example, running errands all over creation and everyone from the produce guy at the grocery store to the office lady at your kids' school asks how you're doing. There are times when you just don't want to get into things. But if you're *not* doing fine—and dealing with something difficult—you can stick your toes in the warm waters of vulnerability and share those difficulties. You can answer, "Yeah, I'm having a hard time with _____" and let the conversation flow from there. You can share your lows as well as your highs with your people.

Is there a risk in sharing this way, in being vulnerable? Absolutely. But nobody has it all together all the time, and when we share our hard stuff, we create a safe space for another to do the same. And doing so increases our sense of belonging with those with whom we share our lives.

God wants us to know that, yes, we need those people who will lower us on a mat, who will move in an inconvenient way on our behalf, speaking truth into us. As true as it is that God works through those listening people in our lives, he also wants us to come directly to him. He is the only One who hears us voice our struggles and fears and weird obsessions and isn't surprised, put out, or inconvenienced—ever. He looks at us not as a hot mess but as his totally beloved. It's safe to say all people will disappoint us at one point or another, but God never will. Our circumstances will, and we will suffer things we want changed. But God will always be moving behind the scenes for our good. So we tell him what's on our mind. We let him affirm our belonging on the inside so we can take the steps we need to belong on the outside in the healthiest way.

Yeah, we shouldn't bare our souls with just anyone. God is always safe, but people are not. Rather, we must prayerfully consider that safe person or three who can be trusted with our honest feelings about what we're going through. We all need people with whom we can share the real struggles as well as the insecurities, the crazy, roll-your-eyes-at-yourself stuff. When we share our hard things, we invite others to do the same and at the same time find a place to belong. Dive deeply with a few and enjoy security in your belonging place around many. Others have been there.

Let them bring you in.

traveling companion: MYSELF

Having lived on this revolving planet for more than forty years, I know the telltale sign that I need to share with someone what's going on inside Kristenville: I spontaneously cry. At what feels like random, even inappropriate, times. *Of course.* When this happens, I know it's time for me to up the vulnerability ante.

I relearned this familiar lesson afresh while visiting friends who were in town for a family reunion. I don't get to see Kelli and Christie very often, so when they invited me for coffee in the afternoon, I immediately said yes.

While I feel I know Kelli and Christie rather well (thank you kindly, internet, for friends made online!), this was only our second time to meet in person. Their sweet mama, Lexie, whom I'd never met before our time together, also joined us.

A few short days prior, our family received difficult news affecting one family member. As is the case with families, what affects one person affects us all. In one way, the event shook our sense of belonging. I felt like I had been shoved into a room with uneven floors and couldn't quite get my bearings. The whole situation was on my mind constantly, and try as I might, I couldn't leave it at home when I left for the coffee date.

As we sat under the whispering cottonwood trees on the patio outside the coffee shop, I talked and chatted with these three lovely ladies. I met Kelli and Christie's darling, chockful-of-personality kiddos. Then Kelli asked me an innocuous question that, unbeknownst to her, directly related to our difficult situation. And right there, over my iced spicy chai latte, I burst into the kind of tears that can't be prettied-up. I mean, I ugly cried like an Olympic pro.

Feeling equal parts horrified and relieved, I gave them an abbreviated rundown of the situation. I rubbed my temples and told them how I was sorry for my embarrassing display, but the situation was so fresh and tender that I just couldn't help it. They listened with true kindness, compassion, and grace as befitted the people they are. They told me there was no need to be sorry. What's more, they shared how, in their own ways, they could totally relate to what I was going through. Eventually the conversation moved on, and I left encouraged and heartened.

More importantly, perhaps, I left knowing I really needed to process the whole shebang more than I had done. I had been talking with my husband, but he needed a break from all 837 of my questions and laments. I had been talking with the Lord too, but I sensed him encouraging me to do the same with trusted sisters, to bring all my inside thoughts, emotions, and reactions to the outside and let him speak life into me through them.

The following day, I shared all my topsy-turvy lows with Aimée at our regularly scheduled coffee date. The next week, I called my friend Allison, who lives in California, and shared with her what was on my mind—the good, bad, and ugly. I scheduled an appointment with Gwen, my counselor, who helps me get underneath things. After talking with them, I felt like a summer breeze had blown off the mountains into my weary heart. My shoulders relaxed as my body released the tension. My clothes seemed to fit less tightly. Those women, my wingwomen, all worked together to give me perspective that while it was well and good to grieve over the loss of one kind of belonging, hope was far from gone.

Vulnerability is hard, yes, but what's hard helps. Because what sits right next to hard is *hope*. Let hope speak to you through the Lord. Let hope speak to you through other loved ones.

Dear one, just let hope speak to you.

~Belong Blessing~

When hard happens and takes away your sense of belonging, may you not feel the pull to cover, conceal, and collapse in silence. When the cold, lonely feelings come, may you not reach for those two words, *I'm fine*, like you would that stretched-out sweater in your closet. Instead, may you stand in the warmth of the bright light of day that comes with sharing your hard stuff with your easy people. May you let them get to you and wrap their warmth around you on the outside as Christ's light fills you from within. And may you relax knowing that, indeed, you do fit in, ugly crying and all.

fourteen

Belonging Isn't for You

Surround yourself with people who speak into you, not about you. Who celebrate your future, not resurrect your past.

Bianca Olthoff

I REMEMBER THAT RAINY, saturated February day when my good friend, the one with much older kids, swung by for a visit when the house looked like we'd been livin' large and cleanin' little. And if you defined "livin' large" as surviving a houseful of sick little people, then living large was what we'd been doing. Answering the doorbell, I shrugged off the state of the house, knowing my friend was no stranger to this stage of life.

As I walked toward the door, I looked down at my baby girl asleep in my arms, body warm and worn out from a persistent virus. I opened the door with one hand and smiled, cocked my head to quietly welcome my friend inside. Shutting the door behind her, I moved to the sofa and cleared off the boys' collection of dinosaurs so we could sit. We chatted quietly for five minutes or so until James and Ethan, finally fever-free, ran hollering into the room. I made my most desperate mom face and shushed them something fierce, pointing to their sleeping sister. The baby woke, and I sighed, exasperated. Swaying with my baby in my arms, I risked a see-through heart and confessed, "You know, some days with little ones are just so hard." I smoothed hair out of my daughter's eyes, blind to my friend's forthcoming response.

"Well, you're the one who decided to have kids. What did you expect?"

I stared at her as her words ricocheted off the walls and hit my heart. *That'll teach me to be vulnerable*, I said to myself.

My mouth shut, and the walls of my heart thickened, because that's what happens when you get a little too real with unsafe people. Instead of giving you understanding and support, they give you the bricks and cement to fashion a false exterior that looks like *I'm fine!* and *Everything's great!* and *Nope, I don't need any help at all.*

I held my sick baby girl close to my hurting heart. My friend left but her words lingered, and I was left wondering what to do with them.

Thinking back on that encounter, close to fifteen years later, I want to wrap my arms around my younger self and say, *The only thing to do is to toss her words away and know they do not belong near you. The only thing to do is know that, at least when it comes to sharing parenting struggles, this woman does not belong in your confidence. On that front, you don't belong with her.*

• • •

As important as it is for us to know where we do belong, it's important for us to know where we *do not*. There are simply some places not meant for us. If, after spending time in someone's company, the scales continually tip toward them questioning our choices and decisions, then we don't belong there. If, like in my story above, a particular relationship hands us more sabotage than support, then let's look ourselves square in our beautiful eyes and tell ourselves: "You don't belong there."

This doesn't mean we only surround ourselves with people who live and think just like us, no sirree. First of all, no one will agree with us on everything. That's as elusive as a happy toddler who hasn't slept in two days. Second of all, of course we're to have people in our lives who can lovingly set us straight. Sometimes it's necessary for us to take our hands away from our ears and experience the rebuke of painful truth. In the end, those words—hard to hear though they may be—are *for* us. Heeding them moves us closer to reflecting the character of Jesus.

That is what makes all the difference: if we repeatedly sense that what another is saying or doing is *not* for us but more for them and their own motives, then we don't belong there. Yeah, we might get a little off track on our back road and need someone to kindly help us find our way on it again. But no one should run us off it into the ditch.

When others desire to be in a relationship with us, they need to show us that our heart is safe in their hands. If it's not, wisdom says we don't let what they say find a way to enter in. We need to pivot from their words rather than let them permeate our minds, hearts, and souls. We need to pivot from toxic to truth.

We never belong where toxicity resides.

A long time ago, the Lord gave me a visual of this, an image of our hearts reflecting the Old Testament tabernacle. This tabernacle represented God's house, the tented palace for Israel's divine King.[1] Here, God dwelled in the midst of the Israelites. It consisted of three primary areas: the outer courtyard, the Holy Place, and the inner Holy of Holies. God was enthroned on what was known as the ark of the covenant in the Holy of Holies, also called the Most Holy Place. The closer one moved inside the tabernacle toward the Holy of Holies, the more valuable the metals used to make items like the lamp, table, and altars became.[2]

Separated by a curtain from the Holy of Holies, the Holy Place was the other room within the tabernacle. It signified God's royal guest room where his people could make a bread offering (known as the bread of presence) declaring God's presence in and provision toward the fruits of their labors.[3]

With an entrance on the east side, the outer courtyard was comprised of curtains and poles that surrounded the other two rooms. While any Israelite could enter the courts, only priests were allowed to enter the Holy Place. Only the high priest could enter into the Holy of Holies. The farther within the tabernacle one moved, the more restricted the access became. It was this way till Jesus's death on the cross of Calvary. Then the curtain between the Holy Place and the Holy of Holies tore in two, granting all people direct access to God (Heb. 10:19–22).

Herein lies the parallel: in our hearts, the entrance, or outer courtyard, is the place where many can come. Other parts are more holy places where people who are *for* us may cross the threshold. And still other parts are for just you and God alone, a Holy of Holies. Don't invite someone into the interior spaces who isn't meant to be there.

If the person speaking to you—be it the little-known coworker in the next cubicle or the well-known family member at Christmas dinner—has not proven a wise, safe voice of wisdom in your life, then refuse to take his or her words to the inner parts of your heart. Don't let someone into your holy place who is kind to you one minute but the next poisons the well against you. You don't belong with anyone who negatively questions your every motive and action.

I wonder too if we'd all do well to resist the urge to overshare, especially when we sense a catch in our spirit telling us not to. Within our culture of laying everything out on social media (I mean, did it really happen if I don't show proof of it on Instagram?), this is harder to do than it used to be. We might just take a giant leap toward feeling like we belonged more if we took a giant leap back by sharing less. Not in an "I'm scared to be vulnerable" way but rather in an "I'll hold this a bit closer and share it with a smaller number of people" way. *Maybe I'll share it with the Lord first and then with a couple of my wingwomen—my safe women who have my back.* We'll do this so we can best set our heart up to receive wisdom rather than condemnation. Toothpaste can't be put back in a tube. Heeding those little nudges and warnings from God about sharing will help us avoid that feeling of wishing we could go back in time and choose differently.

Yeah, every woman struggling to belong needs people she can welcome into that holy place by being vulnerable with them. But if someone isn't safe, it's okay for that person to be on the outside of your heart. No matter the temper tantrum she throws. No matter how she tells you you're hurting her or being unfair to her. Unsafe people and their words do not get inner access to your heart. The end. When they try, picture yourself pivoting away from them and moving toward Truth. Pivoting from their presence puts up a boundary and prevents them from getting free rein to walk beside you on your back road.

• • •

As the Holy of Holies was just for the high priest and the Lord, there may be parts of your story, past and present, best shared with God alone. As the One who knows you better than any person on earth, he will be the only One who speaks to you from a place of flawless for-you truth. As the One who shaped you and saw you and loved you well before your mama laid eyes on you, he will always advise you with your best in mind. He will always bend and curve your back road to belonging in the way that you need, even if that means suggesting boundaries around you so others can't get the access to you they want.

And just as we need to be careful of whom we allow access to our heart, we need to be careful to not take it personally when others don't allow us access to theirs. Likely it's not because we've been careless with their heart. (If we have, Lord, forgive us, and may we consider whether or not we need to apologize to that person as well.) Instead, it's likely because they have limited bandwidth in their day and must tend to who and what the Lord directs is most important. We may even look toward another who is inside someone else's inner place and think, *It should be me, not her.* When you boil it down, God has called the other person there, not you and not me. It's God's best for that person to be there, and it's his best for us to be elsewhere. We can be happy for how God is working in her life while simultaneously being assured he's working the same way in ours.

The Lord may very well keep you on the outside of a person or group as a way of guarding your own heart. As hard as it is to believe this in the moment, sometimes we must accept, as my friend Salena says, that rejection is God's protection from what isn't in our best interest.

As we struggle to hang on to hope for finding where we belong, we can absolutely believe that God hasn't saved his worst for us. We can be *for* ourselves by trusting him to place us with those who will feed, honor, love, and serve us best as we reciprocate those actions to those folks too.

If you are on the outside somewhere, God is simultaneously calling you on the inside somewhere else. You *are* on the inside somewhere else. Remember, there's always room at the table God picks out for you. And since we've committed to not missing those people with whom we're already in, perhaps it's time we committed to not spending large amounts of time bemoaning why we're not at another table. Perhaps it's time we refuse to feel guilty for not inviting those who aren't mindful of caring for our hearts to our own. Perhaps we need to remember that if we have to protect ourselves from those continually *peck peck pecking* us, it's okay to have a boundary so their pointed words remain on the other side of our heart's rooms. If we're going to hide, may it be in the all-compassionate, ever-faithful Jesus Christ— our completely safe place.

traveling companion:
CHELSEA

Several years ago, Chelsea received a mean-spirited letter that let her know in no uncertain terms that she was *out* of a particular group.

That was no conclusion she jumped toward, no ma'am. The letter, written by a longtime friend, actually stated it in black-and-white. It also, however, threw her a single, solitary rope she could use to heft herself back into the gang: she could apologize for everything wrong in that relationship. Chelsea could not only own her own part in the broken relationship but own the other person's part too. The letter went on to call Chelsea hurtful names and bring condemnation to every choice she'd ever made, right down to the school her kids attended and the breakfast food she served her family.

The blunt communication shook Chelsea to her core and made her question where she belonged on every level. But when she thought about it again, she realized there had been a destructive pattern to her relationship with this friend for some time. Chelsea liked helping out this person in a variety of ways and often did so. Periodically, however, she would say no to requests for resources outside her ability to give. Then Chelsea would endure exhausting inquisitions, with her every action and motive questioned. Eventually, their good relationship would be undermined by some "terrible" thing Chelsea had done, and she would feel her heart sink to her ankles as the barrage of criticism ensued.

After receiving that letter, Chelsea knew she could do what she usually did and use that rope to climb, climb, climb up into the other woman's always-changing good graces. But by doing so, she knew it would become a noose that would quickly squeeze the remaining air out of her fragile state of mind over this situation. She knew she didn't belong in this person's life, at least not with the current state of behavior, and her anxiety over every encounter took away her ability to be a present mom and wife to her family—her priority belonging people.

Chelsea had let this friend into her heart's holy place, and it was time to place her in the outer courtyard or beyond.

Still, Chelsea began to wonder that if this friend felt this way—if her accusations were true—might others see the same terrible things?

Needing outside perspective on how to best proceed, Chelsea talked to two people within her own heart's holy place: her husband

and her good friend Amy. Her husband reminded her that God holds her reputation, not her fickle friend. He reminded her she had repeatedly apologized for what she needed to apologize for. If Chelsea had conducted herself in a mature, gracious, and caring manner—which he firmly believed she had—then she could rest knowing no weapon forged against her could stand (Isa. 54:17).

While her husband's steady presence and assurances helped her gain valuable perspective, her friend Amy's words of wisdom at the back of church one Sunday preached an important sermon she needed to hear: sometimes being on the outside is the healthiest place to be. Chelsea immediately felt a peace that comes with knowing that, in this case, being on the outside was indeed best for her. She could evaluate her role in the problems and continue to take ownership of what was hers. However, she could also refuse to hold what the other person needed to own.

With help from her spiritual director, Chelsea thought of her boundary as a closed door but not a bolted one. She could still make herself available for positive, constructive communication, but overt ugliness would no longer be allowed access to her heart. Those who would have access to her heart would be those in her real belonging place: safe family, friends, and Christ.[4]

~Belong Blessing~

When someone tries to bully herself into your life by speaking in a way that dishonors you, may you know her words have no place near you. May the Lord cast them as far as the east is from the west, because there is now no condemnation for those who are in Christ Jesus (Rom. 8:1). May you prayerfully seek not only the best places for you to belong but also wisdom and insight into where you do not. And as you move toward people who support rather than sabotage you, may you be mindful of keeping your heart healthy by allowing only safe people into its rooms, reserving your own holy of holies for just you and God.

fifteen

Speaking Up and Out

Correction does much, but encouragement does more.
Johann Wolfgang von Goethe

MY FAVORITE TEACHER was undoubtedly Mrs. Schatte, my fifth-grade teacher.

Oh, Mrs. Schatte! How she threw love and affection like confetti at us awkward preteens. She was everything my ten-year-old self wanted in a teacher: warm, kind, and interesting. She made her brightly decorated, cozy classroom feel more like a family room than a classroom. She didn't hesitate to take us to task when we deserved it, but she also didn't hesitate to shower us with praise when we deserved it. Without a doubt, she let us know we belonged in her classroom and in this world.

I remember sitting at my desk in her classroom one Friday during a spelling test, right leg folded under my left knee. As was her practice during these tests, Mrs. Schatte would say the word, put it in a sentence, then say the word again. On this particular test, one of her words was "stomach," and Mrs. Schatte said, "Stomach. My stomach will be getting very big in the next several months. Stomach."

I remember biting my lip as I concentrated on spelling out s-t-o-m . . . and then it clicked. It was her way of telling us she would be having a baby, and we lost our minds with squealy excitement. Because she loved us through effervescent encouragement, we were only too happy to return the favor and encourage her right back through our "oooohs" and "aaaahs" and requests to put each of our names in as priority babysitter.

This past winter, I saw Mrs. Schatte for the first time in twenty-five years when I went back to my hometown for my daddy's funeral. When I saw her in the lobby following the service, my mouth dropped open. Not only that, but I immediately teared up. We talked for a good while, and I excitedly introduced her to my kids as my Favorite Teacher of All Time.

Later, I recalled why seeing her affected me so strongly. Mrs. Schatte had noticed the seeds of potential in my young self and watered that potential with encouragement and care. She was one of the first people to tell me I was a good friend to other girls. She was one of the first outside my family to tell me I was a good writer. She saw the good growing in me and named it. On that February day, seeing her beautiful face again connected those dots from young me to adult me, and it raised up a tender place within me. It also brought home this realization: never discount the power of encouraging another. We never know how one small seed of kindness could grow into a sheltering tree. Mrs. Schatte's words were my own sheltering tree, and they helped give me what I needed to do likewise for someone else.

Mrs. Schatte's words and heart showed me pieces of my larger belonging place, and in the process attested to her own belonging place as a life-giving teacher to children.

Proverbs 11:25 says, "Whoever brings blessing will be enriched, and one who waters will himself be watered." Those who water others will have their own belonging place watered. Therefore, if you and

I want to shore up our own belonging, we can encourage another's. Because sometimes the best way to start believing we're in when we feel anything but is to fight feeling with feeling.[1]

My fifth-grade friends and I easily encouraged Mrs. Schatte because she lavishly encouraged us. It's harder to do the same with someone who doesn't necessarily encourage you back. It's doubly harder to encourage the one who brings out feelings of inferiority or even jealousy. But the closer those feelings creep, the more we need to do something opposite, like specifically seeking out that person to encourage them.

It's mighty hard to be jealous of someone we're cheering on at the same time, isn't it? Negative feelings stemming from comparison multiply in the dark. Using the light of encouragement to speak against negative feelings makes them disappear as it brightens our mood and our heart.

• • •

A woman in the Bible you may be acquainted with, Elizabeth, could have taught a class in this. A devoted wife to her husband, she became pregnant the same time her peers held grandbabies. She had what today's doctors would call a "geriatric pregnancy." Elizabeth decided to play it safe and spend the first several months of her nine-month journey in seclusion. She wasn't going to take any unnecessary chances when it came to this miracle baby. She would put her feet up whenever her body demanded and schedule allowed.

At one point during Elizabeth's pregnancy, her much younger cousin, who also happened to be pregnant, came to visit. When teenage Mary entered her house, Elizabeth knew this was no ordinary familial visit. No, ma'am. Because as Mary greeted her cousin, Elizabeth's baby bounced up and down inside her. It was as if Elizabeth's baby could not contain his excitement over the visitor—or rather, visitors.

Elizabeth, upon hearing Mary's friendly, "Hello, cousin!" didn't waste a moment with small talk or idle chitchat.

And Elizabeth was filled with the Holy Spirit, and she exclaimed with a loud cry, "Blessed are you among women, and blessed is the fruit of your womb! And why is this granted to me that the mother of my Lord should come to me? For behold, when the sound of your greeting came to my ears, the baby in my womb leaped for joy. And blessed is she who believed that there would be a fulfillment of what was spoken to her from the Lord." (Luke 1:41–45)

Three times Elizabeth called a blessing upon Mary. From a place of total humility, Elizabeth lifted Mary up over and over again. "You are a blessing! Your baby is a blessing! What have I done to get the privilege of *you* visiting me? Bless you again for the good choices you've made!" Elizabeth celebrated Mary's belonging place as the Savior's mother through a steady stream of beautiful, life-giving affirmation and encouragement.

Elizabeth could've let jealousy and comparison rule the day. She could've been all-out annoyed that this young'un had swooped in to flaunt her pregnancy with the baby Son of God. She could've said—or at least thought—*You would have to one-up me here and throw a rain cloud on my own good news! You would have to spoil my own miracle!* She could've chosen to try to put a damper on Mary's God-given belonging place by pushing away her relationship with Mary. But she didn't.

Instead, she affirmed Mary's belonging place, and in turn that affirmed her own belonging place as one benefiting from the Savior Mary would birth. It also affirmed her belonging place because it showed how she fit in as one to speak blessing from a place of humility. Any time a woman wanting to belong helps another see all the ways *she* belongs, that woman stands in a place of humility as she builds another up. And standing in a place of humility is a back road where one always belongs.

By encouraging Mary, Elizabeth encouraged herself. The same goes for you and me: encouraging others will encourage ourselves. It's the not-so-subtle nudge that sends jealousy and comparison over our own belonging places running up Pike's Peak. It's one surefire way to take the spotlight off our own pity party over where we wish we belonged and put it on the celebration of where God has placed us.

With the help of the Holy Spirit, Elizabeth securely sat in her belonging place. Through her lavish encouragement to Mary, we know she didn't dwell on what she didn't have. She didn't compare and despair. She felt thankful for what she had, and because of her humility and gratitude she could openly and honestly thank God for what Mary had too.

• • •

If I ask you to call to mind someone right now whose blessings and good things run parallel to yours yet you perceive her outcomes to be more desirable destinations, who would that person be? I can think of my someone. If we call that person to mind and consider her current belonging place, do we have a hard time being happy for her? Do we compare and despair?

One reason the compare and despair trap happens is because hoarding encouragement weighs us down. We can release that pressure by speaking life directly into the one we keep comparing ourselves to. We can replace envy with encouragement.

Does this feel like an impossible task? If so, I get it. But we don't have to pull the encouragement from a source inside ourselves. We can get it directly from God.

> Now may the God who gives endurance and encouragement grant
> you to live in harmony with one another, according to Christ Jesus,
> so that you may glorify the God and Father of our Lord Jesus Christ
> with one mind and one voice. (Rom. 15:5–6 CSB)

God gives us encouragement and the endurance to offer encouragement to another. So if you feel tired, spent, and just too annoyed at a person to encourage her, pray for God's help. God, who can't help but give good stuff to his kids, will faithfully give you what you don't have on your own so you may speak up and out toward another. Like any of us mamas who want our kids to get along, God wants to empower us to get along with one another too.

Let's pray for the Holy Spirit's help to get our hearts from where they are to where they need to be. Let's pray that he gives us eyes to see how we can encourage that person, whether she's easy to encourage or difficult, specifically in her own job, callings, and life. And then let's offer a prayer of thanks that God is doing his thing for her just as he's doing his thing for you and me.

It's a small detail in her life, yes, but it's the small details that make the difference.

Proverbs 12:25 says, "Anxiety in a man's heart weighs him down, but a good word makes him glad." Most of us have been in a heavy, anxious place before and can think of a time when another's encouraging words lifted us up. While I've certainly been there, sometimes when I'm in an anxious place it feels more like I have a hundred balloons floating around inside of me, and I need something to tether them down in one place, something to hold on to. A well-placed word of encouragement from another does this for me.

As we walk our own back road to belonging, our job is to simply hold the hand of Christ and not worry about the specifics of the journey. Put on the blinders that help you share and prepare, not compare and despair. Speak words that make people stronger, even if some folks never say thank you. Speak words that prepare others for their God-given jobs. Speak words that prepare you to fully belong where you're supposed to belong.

> So speak encouraging words to one another. Build up hope so you'll all be together in this, no one left out, no one left behind. I know you're already doing this; just keep on doing it. (1 Thess. 5:11 Message)

Speak encouraging words to one another. Paul echoes the Lord's heart when he commands it, because it's for our benefit as much as the receiver's.

When you feel like you don't belong, get yourself in the middle of some intentional encouragement giving. Be a give-courager. Pull back the curtain a little and let another person see who is on her side. Who's rooting for her. Holding her up.

Don't hold the words in, dear one. See others and name their good things. And let God settle you into your belonging place a little more.

traveling companion:
LAUREN

In the 1980s, Lauren worked in the publishing industry in New York City. At that time, her daily trek from home to office to home again brought her in regular contact with at least a hundred homeless people along the way. Some of the folks she passed on the streets and sidewalks suffered from mental illness, others from drug addiction, and still others from lost opportunities. As she walked past those men and women, she would feel the whole gamut of emotions— heartbroken and fearful, compassionate and overwhelmed.

One dark night, Lauren walked home from work later than usual. The air was especially damp and cold, so she looked forward to the warmth waiting beyond her own front door. She was just around the corner from home when she saw him: a homeless man wearing no coat but standing with wobbly crutches. He shivered as he held out his coffee cup and asked passersby for spare change.

For a few reasons, Lauren didn't want to stop. She was cold and tired, and she'd already stopped to give money to other folks. Just the same, as she approached this man, she began rummaging through her purse in search of whatever change she had left. As she did so, the fellow began talking to her.

"Ya know, the shelters are so crowded, it's hard to get a comfortable place there," he said.

Lauren gave him brief eye contact and replied, "Oh, yeah?" before looking once again for the elusive change.

"Yeah, and I used to have a coat, but someone stole it when I was at the shelter," he responded.

Lauren shook her purse, hoping to reveal a few coins. "Oh no, that's really too bad," she answered, listening less to him and more for the sound of jingling coins. Finally, Lauren spied some quarters, gathered them in her palm, and let them fall with a *clink, clink, clink* into the man's cup.

And then he spoke words that Lauren has never been able to forget: "Hey, thanks for this, and thanks for talking to me."

As Lauren walked the rest of the way home, she thought about how she didn't have any real conversation with the homeless man. All she did was stop, look him in the eye, and give him a few words along with her change. But in giving him these simple things, she validated him and helped him know he was seen.

That moment twenty-five years ago forever changed how Lauren acknowledged the homeless. Each person is a human being with a need to be seen. While it was impossible for her to give money or resources to every single person in need, she could look those she passed in the eye and tell them, "Hello," or "I'm so sorry." She realized that, to those men and women, those small actions were more valuable than money.

Like Lauren, you and I can't help every person in need who crosses our path. But we can look them in the eye and acknowledge them with a smile or a kind, short word. By doing this, we validate each person. Those are simple things, but as we know, the simple things make up the big, important things. The simple things encourage—and give courage—to the receiver.

In God's less-is-more, down-is-up way of leading us, what we give becomes the foundation for what we receive. It's up to us to trust God enough to believe that if we first spend a little of ourselves, we'll secure something for ourselves: a greater way to belong.

~Belong Blessing~

May you have the courage to plant seeds of encouragement into the heart of another. May you feel God's unabashed pleasure every time you make another soul stronger, and may you in turn feel your own soul's belonging secured all the more. May you follow Elizabeth's example of choosing blessing over comparison and jealousy. And may you find yourself standing in the sunlit encouragement you share as it illuminates far beyond where you hoped or imagined it would. Be a light and know you belong.

Part III

Inviting

Bringing another in.

sixteen

Being Belong-Makers

The daily notice of our alliance was both muted and essential:
we were the lattice that made room for the rose.

Gail Caldwell, *Let's Take the Long Way Home*

DURING ONE STICKY LATE-SUMMER MONTH of August, the
military moved my family of five from an arid, bone-dry desert to
the humid, green-o-rama landscapes of the Midwest. We bought a
house within the school district we wanted our kids to attend, an
'80s split-level home absent of charm but encircled with beautiful,
sky-reaching trees. Fall came soon after we moved in, and boy howdy
did James and Ethan, our five-year-old twins, go hog wild in all the
leaves. They'd rake them in a pile then hoot and holler as they jumped
and dive-bombed into them.

One day, as James and Ethan enjoyed their leaf-loving antics in the
pile by our curb, they moved ever-closer to our neighbor's own big
pile of leaves. As they did so, I was working on the side of the house,
removing weeds from flower beds while their little sister napped.

Suddenly, I heard a commotion from the front of the house. I walked around the corner just in time to see my two preschoolers staring wide-eyed at our eighty-three-year-old neighbor.

Pointing her shaky finger at the boys, she bellowed, "You boys get outta my leaves right now! You hear me? You get outta those leaves and don't mess with them anymore!"

James and Ethan, eyes big as turkey platters, nodded their heads up and down. I walked over to our neighbor and told her how sorry I was for the mess they'd made. I directed the boys to the garage where our rakes waited for them to use to tidy up her piles. She gave an exasperated *humph!* and slowly turned around to walk back into her house. As I watched her go, I knew her sour mood could be somewhat justified—no telling how long it took her to rake those piles.

Now, we've had cranky neighbors before (shout-out to the senior neighbors in Hawaii who nearly called the police on my kids for riding bikes in front of their property). My natural inclination this time was to do what I'd done before: give her a mile-wide berth. But this time I felt the Lord ask me to do something different. I felt him say, *Reach out to her.* I'm sure he'd asked me to do it before with others; however, this time I listened. And with the enthusiasm one has for stepping barefoot on an anthill, I began to think of ways I could reach toward her.

A month later, the kids and I made some cinnamon pumpkin bread, wrapped up a few slices of it on a plate, and took it to her front door. After we rang the doorbell and she answered, I introduced myself and the kids. She let the smallest smile show and said her name was Mary. She accepted our homemade offering politely and said thank you before we told her goodbye and to have a good day. A short time later we brought her chocolate chip cookies, and she invited us inside her house. We sat and talked over her too-loud TV, and I silently prayed for the kids to behave and show her their sweet side. Still mindful of not overstaying our welcome *or* her good graces, after a few minutes I gathered the kids, thanked her for her hospitality, and headed back home.

Throughout winter and into spring and summer, we continued to reach out to Ms. Mary (as the kids called her). We invited her over for Christmas dinner. We planted flowers in pots the kids painted and took them to her house. The kids drew her pictures, and I baked her brownies. Every time we dropped something off, she'd invite us in her home. Eventually, her marble exterior cracked, and we saw her softer side.

While we invited Ms. Mary to our house many times, she always declined. We offered to help her with household chores, but she told us not to worry about it. She and I never explored the waters below shallow small talk, unless it was to comment on whatever aired on her TV. All in all, I never sensed we did that much for her except feed her sweet tooth and give her a little company.

However, a phone message she left us a couple of years later proved me wrong.

Shortly after New Year's, we returned home after making the nine-hundred-mile drive to Oklahoma to visit family for Christmas. After helping unload the car, I checked our answering machine for messages (this was the olden days of the early 2000s). The last message, from Ms. Mary, had been left only two days before we returned home. She'd had a sudden health crisis, and she called to tell us she wouldn't be leaving the hospital. Her final words on the machine were, "I just thought you'd like to know what was going on, Kristen. Please tell the kids I love them. I love you, and I hope to see you later."

Ms. Mary had died the very next day, and I cried thinking how we'd missed saying goodbye by only twenty-four hours.

In the grand scheme of things, I'd done so little for her. Yet it was enough to make her feel loved. In a way only Jesus can do, that call proved that my anemic fish and less-than-stellar loaves could somehow turn into a belonging place for Ms. Mary.

That is the way of the back road, though. We bring little to nothing, and Jesus brings the rest. Jesus makes it make a difference.

I still tear up when I think about it, because as we brought Ms. Mary into our family circle, she brought us into the neighborhood circle. We'd moved to a new town in a new state where we knew very few people, and reaching out to Ms. Mary helped me find a belonging place within my new neck of the woods. With a husband who worked long hours and three wee-watts in my care, I found that meeting with Ms. Mary opened the door for me to befriend other neighbors too, further helping me feel like I belonged in that neighborhood full of outdated split-levels.

• • •

If I had let that first unfavorable encounter with Ms. Mary be the beginning and end of our interaction, all of this would have been different. The Lord taught me then and there my biggest lesson for securing my own sense of belonging: what helps most of all is thinking of myself as a belong-maker. Because bringing creates belonging.

Just as encouraging another in his or her belonging place encourages us in ours, bringing another in will make a belonging place for us too. Becoming a belong-maker doesn't mean big displays of high-pressure socialization. In fact, the back road way is considering what small, largely unseen things we can do to bring someone in. Heaven knows, our family didn't do anything grand for Ms. Mary. We simply showed up with a smile and sometimes with treats. That was enough.

Matthew 6:6 tells us: "But when you pray, go into your room and shut the door and pray to your Father who is in secret. And your Father who sees in secret will reward you." Some had been praying in public in order to be seen, and to that action the Lord said that "they have received their reward" (v. 5). These verses confirm it's those places—those hidden places only God sees—that hold opportunities for special rewards. One of the rewards wrapped up in these small, noticed-only-by-a-few actions is a deeper knowledge of our belonging.

As you and I practice vulnerability by welcoming a safe, trusted loved one into our hearts, we can take that next step to invite another into our home. Ms. Mary didn't take us up on our offer for this, but others have. As I've invited someone over for coffee on my porch or dinner at my table, bringing that friend in has created belonging for myself as well. Not every time, of course. As we've learned, there are times we meet with folks and discover where we don't belong. But that doesn't deter us from trying again with someone else, from opening our front door and offering what we have—even if it's just coffee or store-bought goodies—to the one the Lord nudges us toward.

Sometimes we're called to serve across oceans, yes. That is valued and needed, no question. Other times we're called to simply serve across our hometown, the railroad tracks, or the backyard fence. Small gestures offered repeatedly become habits of hospitality. And doing so also becomes one sense of belonging: a habit that anchors each of us to a healthier, happier place of living *and* blessing.

> How blessed are you who enter into these things,
>   you men and women who embrace them. . . .
> Make sure no outsider who now follows GOD
>   ever has occasion to say, "GOD put me in second-class.
>   I don't really belong,"
> And make sure no physically mutilated person
>   is ever made to think, "I'm damaged goods.
>   I don't really belong." (Isa. 56:2–3 Message)

One of the biggest gifts we can give another person is the gift of being seen. We create belonging for ourselves when we make another feel known in some small way. Whether someone in our circle wears scars we can see or a slew of wounds we can't, we want to be one who gives her cause to say, "I belong." We want to enter into the place where she feels seen and known by us, because that will lead her to the place where she feels seen and known by her Creator. When we enter into that place, we enter into God's blessing.

• • •

Like you, I can remember a time when someone's brush-off made me feel second class. It was as if their action yelled through a megaphone, *You don't belong near me*. And while it's no fun to think about, I've also been guilty of making another feel like she didn't belong because she didn't serve me or my purposes well in that moment. I'm guilty of not bringing another in because I didn't want to take the time or expend the energy God asked me to give. I've said no to him and thereby said no to the blessing. I've acted like I'm the apple of my own eye.

Because God loves us and doesn't want us to run ourselves ragged serving ourselves into the ground, he doesn't ask us to be Chief Belong-Maker for Every Person We Know. No, no, no. But in various seasons of our lives, he does ask us to be a belong-maker for a few. He asks us, in one way or another, to give a cup of cold water to another (Mark 9:41). And he does it with the end goal of not punishing us but blessing us as we bless another.

During Sunday school one day, our teacher, Luke, said something I haven't been able to get out of my mind. He said, "Sometimes we want the crown without the cross." Yeah, it's true for me. I want the reward without the work. There's no getting around it: being a belong-maker brings an element of work, much more so than what is required to double-tap an Instagram photo or like a Facebook post.

Jesus, more than any other human on the planet, put in the work as a belong-maker. Of course, his saving work on the cross brought us all *in*. He also paved the way for us to follow as belong-makers, to do the work of being there for others. He knew where he belonged: walking the dirt-caked roads of the world with his messy, broken people. Because he did so, every one of us has a belonging place.

Finding our place and our people does not happen in a unicorns-falling-from-the-sky magical way. However, after we put in the work of being a belong-maker for our few, then we will get the miracle: the unique-to-us plan that God knows we need to belong as he created us to belong. Dietrich Bonhoeffer said:

> Christ walks on earth as your neighbor as long as there are people. He walks on the earth as the one through whom God calls you, speaks to

you and makes his demands. . . . Christ stands at the door. He lives in the form of the person in our midst.[1]

Release expectations, give first, then receive Jesus in your midst. Receive the blessing of belonging.

Traveling companion: MYSELF

My family and I were new members of a church, and its large size meant it was much harder to get to know people. Even our Sunday school class spilled over our meeting space. So, in two distinct ways, I decided to create an environment that made it easier to get to know some of the other gals in the class.

First, I invited a spunky brunette named Aimée over for coffee and pie on my back porch. I didn't even make the coffee but happily pointed her in the direction of our Keurig and assortment of coffee flavors. While our daughters hung out in the house, Aimée and I hung out on my "vintage" Walmart patio furniture and talked parenting problems, shared experiences as former military wives, and our mutual dislike of snow in April (thanks, Colorado!). We sipped warm coffee and drank in warm conversation. When the gathering ended, we both felt we'd reached a place where we came alive a bit more.

Buoyed by that one-on-one conversation, I decided to expand the idea of being a belong-maker and asked some other gals from Sunday school to stop by for a grown-up tea party (because I'm ninety on the inside). Since I'd already had Aimée over, I knew at least one person a bit better. Plus, Aimée is able to talk easy-breezy with just about anyone. Conversation ninjas like Aimée are a blessed bridge between yourself and the awkwardness that comes with hanging out with others you don't know too well.

And so, a few weeks later, the six ladies I'd invited to my home sipped Earl Grey and strawberry pomegranate tea with me, and we fed ourselves on cucumber dill sandwiches and classic scones. Just to give the gathering a little direction, I decided to make it a "book exchange tea party." Every person brought a book or two they didn't mind trading, and we each went home with at least one new book as well. We had a little bit of everything—mysteries, sci-fi, devotionals, and other fiction and nonfiction. Each person gave a short synopsis of the books she'd brought and told us why she liked them. Then, after drawing numbers, each person picked which new books she wanted to take home. We ate, sipped, talked, and got to know each other a bit better, and I got to feel like I belonged within my church a little more.

Now, before you write me off because you believe a tea party sounds about as appealing to you as hosting a posse of frat boys after a football game, know that I really, *really* dig a tea party. I love the tea flavors and the treats. I love the china. I love the way it encourages me to sit down and slow down. But if that isn't your thing, then become a belong-maker in the environment that *is* your thing. I use what I like to do—baking, fixing tea, and reading books—to make the experience more fun and less work. I fall on the introverted side, so I'm not afraid of using parameters to prevent myself from never having people over. I'll let those who offer to bring something do so. I'll have a start *and* end time to the festivities. I'll make one of my tried-and-true recipes so I don't have to think too much about what to serve.

Having Aimée over for pie and conversation was only the first of many get-togethers, and she is one of my dearest friends today. Hosting the book-lover's tea provided an atmosphere for more conversation and helped me get to know several ladies better than before. But first I had to risk the vulnerability—and do a wee bit of work—that comes with opening my home to others.

~Belong Blessing~

May you have your heart tuned to the direction the Lord leads you to be a belong-maker. As you open up your heart and home to another, may you know the grace notes of Christ are affirming in you the deeper, uniquely true-for-you song of your belonging place. And as you do the work of welcoming in your few, may you know blessing will follow, because God always keeps his promises.

seventeen

Going There Anyway

The devil only gives two options: black or white. Republican or
Democrat. My group or your group. There's a third option. Us.

Miles McPherson

As we consider how to enhance our own belonging by
bringing another in, could we consider someone who is different
from us, even *very* different from us? Because sometimes the thing
you don't expect to bring you *in* is exactly what does.

Former first lady Jackie Kennedy learned this in an unexpected way
after visiting the White House in February 1971. At that time, the
current first lady, Pat Nixon, invited Jackie and her children, Caroline, age thirteen, and John, age ten, to come to the White House for
the official unveiling of former President and First Lady Kennedy's
portraits. Custom dictated the former first family would attend and
watch the unveiling. However, such unveilings were often public, and
Jackie wasn't up for a large, official ceremony. Jackie and her children
hadn't visited the White House since their husband and father's assas-
sination seven and a half years earlier. Jackie let Pat know that, under

certain terms, she and her kids would attend a private viewing of the unveiling, but not a public one.

On February 3, the Nixons welcomed the Kennedys to the White House without the slightest fanfare. Pat made certain Jackie's terms of the visit were kept down to the letter, especially regarding its privacy. The meeting wasn't noted on any calendar, and for its duration the White House stayed on lockdown. What's more, no foot traffic was allowed in the typically busy corridors near the viewing.

Pat and her twentysomething daughters, Tricia and Julie, did what they could to make the visit a relaxing one for their guests. Tricia and Julie gave Caroline and John a partial tour of places they'd frequented when they lived in the White House. They invited the Kennedy children to play with their dogs along the way. Pat, knowing that Jackie's restoration of the White House meant a great deal to her, talked with Jackie about the new antiques she'd added to various collections.

After viewing Jackie's portrait, the time came to see President Kennedy's portrait. Jackie and the children viewed it quietly. Caroline and John told their mother how much they liked it, and Jackie thanked them for hanging her husband's picture in a prominent place. The Nixons and Kennedys concluded their time together by having dinner in the Family Dining Room.

Upon returning home to New York, John, Caroline, Jackie, and even Jackie's mother-in-law, Rose Kennedy, all wrote thank-you notes to Pat and her family. Jackie's own words to the Nixon family showed just how meaningful the trip was to her:

> Can you imagine the gift you gave us to return to the White House privately with my little ones while they are still young enough to rediscover their childhood. . . . The day I always dreaded turned out to be one of the most precious ones I have spent with my children. May God bless you all. Most gratefully, Jackie.[1]

Understandably, Jackie had dreaded the day she would have to go back to the White House. She likely expected it to be difficult in every way, yet Pat Nixon's thoughtfulness and sensitivity turned it into a day of fond remembrance. The Nixons listened to Jackie's requests and humbled themselves to welcome her and her children into the White House in the way the former first family needed, so the Kennedys left the White House feeling glad they'd come.

Because Pat and her daughters held a belong-maker attitude toward their visitors, the thing Jackie didn't expect to bring her and her children in was exactly what did.

Considering the visit as an adult, Caroline later recalled,

> I think [my mother] really appreciated Mrs. Nixon's thoughtfulness in the sense that there are family values and a dedication to politics and patriotism that go beyond any disagreement on issues or party. One of the things you learn, having lived in the White House, is that there really are these common experiences, and what we share is so much larger than what divides us.[2]

• • •

Reaching out in kindness. Responding with gentleness. Putting ourselves in someone else's position in an attempt to see life from their vantage point. Considering someone as a person rather than a platform or ideology. This is what belong-makers do. Granted, it's easier to bring another in when that person looks and thinks similarly to us. But what if they look different? Sound different? Are from different parts of the world? Vote differently than you?

Yeah, this is the truth: I'm guilty of writing off friendship with folks who are different from me. I've had folks write off friendship with me for the same reason. After I married my military man and transferred to a new college in Ohio, one person heard my thick-as-August-humidity Okie accent and declared, "I generally find all people with Southern accents kinda dumb." Well.

But in my own way, I'm guilty of the same.

Perhaps, like me, you can think of how you've rounded up people and summed up their character or intellect based on one fact.

I generally find people with _____ kind of dumb.

I generally find people who vote _____ totally clueless.

I generally find people who believe _____ rather stupid.

I'm ashamed to admit it, but I've filled in those blanks with an assortment of qualifiers.

We may write off real friendship with someone because he or she seems too different. Whether the differences are ethnic, social, political, in personality, or all the above, we've shied away from a person because we're not so sure what we'd talk about. At other times we shy away from someone different from us because that person reminds us of someone we'd like to be but aren't.

It's not that you and I only seek friends who are exactly like us. No. Rather, we don't go looking for friends whose differences make us uncomfortable, insecure, or afraid. At least, I don't necessarily go looking for them.

But you know what?

I just need to go there anyway. I need to look beyond her differences and into her eyes and see the heart, the person made in God's image. I need to remember heaven is going to be a mosaic of differences. I need to see what I can do to bring a little of heaven to my corner of earth by welcoming differences. Because while moving through uncomfortable parts of differences can last a little while, the rewards of a richer, deeper relationship because of those differences can last a lifetime.

You and I have several biblical road maps for putting this into action too.

Consider Jesus's disciples, a diverse, ragtag group with varying personalities that included educated scholars, lowly fishermen, and a despised tax collector.

Consider Jesus's parable about how a Samaritan, a member of a group hated by the Jewish people, helped a Jewish man who had been beaten and left for dead.

Consider contemplative Mary and get 'er done Martha, two sisters who lived together and served the Lord in their unique ways.

Consider how God specializes in making the impossible possible, and how his good things spring up from the very place you'd never expect. (Here's looking at you, terrorist Saul-turned-apostle-Paul.)

I forget this, however. I expect my relationships to fit together like a puzzle—but as we've talked about before, we're more mosaic than puzzle. Like grout holds tile pieces in place, we need Christ's love to enter all the in-between places and hold our relationships together. That's just what he does: he binds together what otherwise might not fit. Jesus, who died and rose for one and all, is the substance of all that matters (Col. 2:17). He makes the tricky-together work in harmony. Then, when we stand back to take a look, we're amazed at the picture of heaven staring back at us.

The most delightful relationships made along our back road may take us to uncomfortable places. They stretch our faith. God plants us in community not only to accomplish this but also to expose our blind spots. Iron sharpens iron, and our dullness disappears when our weaknesses find renewed strength in others' stories and examples. When we humble ourselves to learn from one another's life experiences and perspectives, we find ourselves within a strong, diverse tapestry of community that benefits all its members.

Holley Gerth once told me, "Awkward is the price of admission for authentic connection." Amen, amen. Yeah, there's no getting over the awkward factor anytime we connect with new people, whether they're super similar or super unfamiliar to us. But it's a short bridge between awkward and awesome on our own back roads, and we can put one foot in front of the other and cross the thing. When we arrive at a richer, more fulfilling belonging place, we'll be so glad we went there anyway.

traveling companions:
SALENA AND MYSELF

While speaking at a function for US Army and Air Force spouses in Colorado Springs, I met a most delightful woman named Salena. She was kind and warm, and as I gave my talk I enjoyed her animated feedback from the audience in the form of "Yes!" and "Amen!"

At least one person is picking up what I'm dropping, I thought to myself.

After my talk ended and the participants were milling about, I introduced myself to her and found myself immediately at ease with her sincere, effervescent demeanor. We did the small-talk thing for a few short minutes and then I deep-dived by asking her a question that set the tone for our relationship still today.

At that time, our country's national headlines focused on deep racial division, highlighted by altercations between police officers and young African American men. These headlines weighed on my mind something fierce. I had thoughts on the subject, but I knew my own perspective couldn't be the beginning and end of the conversation. To say it was would mean pride and hard-heartedness ruled the day, and I didn't want to be a part of that.

As I sat there chatting with Salena, I felt the Lord telling me she was a safe person to ask my awkward questions. Since Salena herself is African American, I was deeply curious about her perspective. So, at a break in the conversation, I said, "Salena, I have a personal question for you, and if you're not comfortable answering, then I totally understand."

She nodded, and I took that as encouragement to keep going.

"Could you help me understand what is going on concerning the headlines and the racial division in our country?"

Salena gave me straight-up answers to my straight-up questions, and I devoured them. She gave me her story, both her history and her present. We didn't solve any big issues that night. But after listening to her, I moved closer to understanding a bigger picture of why things are the way they are.

Until then, I'd never initiated an uncomfortable, prickly conversation with someone I'd just met. I'm not big on small talk anyway, but still, on an unassuming Friday night, there are topics you don't want to sidle up next to. But Salena did indeed prove to be a safe person to share with, and that night we talked for over two hours about the headlines, our lives as military spouses, our families, and everything in between.

Since then, we've done the same a hundred times over. We get together for coffee and talk about the easy stuff, like where she got her shimmery scarlet lipstick. We talk about the not-so-easy stuff, like race relations. We have dinner together with our spouses, during which we talk about everything from parenting teens to affirmative action. We go there, there, and *there*. We don't always agree, but we listen respectfully and value each other's perspective. As is true in any friendship, we don't have to agree on everything to get along.

Here's the really interesting part: while we frequently talk about uncomfortable subjects together, it isn't uncomfortable to do so. It's not! I think that's because of a few reasons. First, Salena continues to be a safe place where I can lay my questions down, and she says I've been the same for her. Second, we ask each other hard questions with the clear goal of understanding the other's perspective—not airing our own Big Important Opinions. That Friday night long ago, she graciously—not defensively—answered my questions with gentleness and honesty. But before any of that happened, I had to cross the awkward bridge on my own back road to belonging toward her.

Traveling the back road through that initially uncomfortable conversation was a path that led to one of my most favorite belonging places: my friendship with Salena. And now I can't imagine my life without her.

~Belong Blessing~

As you travel your own back road to belonging, may God bring you to a place of unexpected blessings by way of an unexpected encounter. May you be able to look past the awkward and see the amazing that could be found in that unforeseen encounter. And as you get to know someone with whom you see a difference or two, may grace, understanding, and listening ears be the order of the day as you walk your back road to a more profound belonging place.

eighteen

Persevering on the Path

You're winning the battle—when you stay in the battle.

Ann Voskamp

I, FOR ONE, GET MIGHTY DISCOURAGED about finding my belonging place when it takes longer than I want. Like a cantankerous toddler, I want what I want, and I want it *now*.

You know what I mean?

You invite people to your podcast or blog, and no one shows up.

You ask that sweet gal to join you for coffee, and she has another excuse.

You try to start a book club, but no one has room in their schedule.

You plan a well-thought-out vacation with extended family, and nobody can make the timing work.

You start a nonprofit and would sooner get a pig to volunteer to be the main course at a barbecue than get a donor to volunteer at your event.

You're doing all the "right" things, but you can't get others to make room for you right now. Your heart is willing and able to be a belong-maker, and you're looking inside and outside the usual avenues to find your place and your people. But sometimes, our suggestions for getting together will be met with rejection. Or, like my playdate luncheon I told you about in the introduction, we bravely open up our home to others and no one shows up. What are you to do when that happens?

It's simple, really: try again. It's much less likely we'll find our place of belonging if we give up searching altogether.

When our overtures of hospitality are met with something less than enthusiasm, it is tempting to cross our arms, say "fine" through clenched teeth, and shut and bolt our front door. But we can't let this setback stop us from looking for our own meaningful belonging places. We need to shake the dust off our boots and try again.

It's always worth it—we're always worth it—to keep on keepin' on our back road to belonging. Any lasting back road is bordered with the strongest of materials: perseverance.

One thing that might happen as we keep on moving down our back road is that we'll experience the Lord's work in a way that, to be frank, won't make a lick of sense at the time. He'll move in a way we're certain is his will for us, but it also looks plumb crazy from our vantage point. Maybe we invested a lot of work in something to move us to a stronger sense of belonging, and though those efforts seemed to be on target, they inexplicably crumbled. Or perhaps we found a place that seemed to make total sense, but it got ripped to shreds, and what we were left with made zero sense on paper. All our expectations and desires for belonging where we thought we'd belong melted away like ice on the pavement in July.

We throw our hands up in the air and cry out, "Why did—how could—this happen? I thought I was in, or at least close to being in.

And now the only thing I'm 'in' is a hot mess. I'm further away than ever from where I want to be."

• • •

Not long ago, something life-altering happened to one of my friends that drove this home for me. This loved one experienced a personal loss that culminated in the demise of a long-held dream. She expected to be knee-deep in her own belonging place, but it was not to be. The Lord moved in such an obviously profound way against it that she had no possible course of action but to abandon her plan altogether. It was a huge change in direction, and it made little sense at the time.

As I talked with her about this, she said something to me I've not forgotten. While processing this abrupt left turn on her path, she sensed the Lord saying to her heart, *I know it's heartbreaking to be in this place right now, and it's not the place you want to be. But trust that I'm saving you from a bigger heartbreak down the road.*

When she wanted to ask all the *why* questions, the Lord gave her a *what* answer. She used that as a springboard for questions that could help her persevere toward her belonging place.

What is the Lord teaching me as I walk along this unknown part of my back road?

What new alternatives do I need to consider?

What good things might I find along the way?

At a time when her circumstances didn't seem to make much sense, these questions helped her persevere as she waited for the Lord to make her place known. They have also helped her abandon all her makes-sense ideas of where she thought she belonged for where the Lord would ask her to belong—wherever that turned out to be.

Jesus's disciple Peter could relate. He faced an unexpected change in direction, right out of the blue. As told in Luke 5, Peter and other fishermen were cleaning their nets after an unsuccessful fishing trip on a lake. As they scrubbed their supplies, Jesus got in one of the boats, which belonged to Peter, and began teaching the crowd assembled around him on the shore. When he finished speaking, Jesus and Peter (then called Simon) conversed.

> [Jesus] said to Simon, "Put out into the deep and let down your nets for a catch." And Simon answered, "Master, we toiled all night and took nothing! But at your word I will let down the nets." (Luke 5:4–5)

I love that Simon Peter allowed himself the freedom to question Jesus. Because haven't most of us, at one time or another, questioned what the Lord has asked us to do? Jesus, a teacher and a carpenter's kid, was not an experienced fisherman like Peter. If Peter had worked all night to catch fish, he probably did all the right things to increase his chances of a successful haul. Clearly, the conditions were not favorable for a good catch. How many of us would have the gumption to tell someone in a field of expertise way outside our own how to do his or her job? Doing so would be impertinent at best and just plain crazy at worst. How can we advise or speak into what we don't know about?

Yet Jesus knew what Peter needed.

Peter questioned him, but in the end answered his request anyway. His reward for obeying Jesus was the catch of a lifetime.

> And when they had done this, they enclosed a large number of fish, and their nets were breaking. They signaled to their partners in the other boat to come and help them. And they came and filled both the boats, so that they began to sink. But when Simon Peter saw it, he fell down at Jesus' knees, saying, "Depart from me, for I am a sinful man, O Lord." For he and all who were with him were astonished at the catch of fish that they had taken. (vv. 6–9)

By faith, Peter did as the Lord asked and received more than his boat could hold. Peter and the other fishermen followed Jesus's crazy, this-doesn't-make-sense advice and reaped unheard-of results. They first trusted him, *then* they saw the reward. Faith came before the fruit. Peter also saw himself a little more clearly, believing he didn't deserve such plentiful gifts. In his eyes he wasn't good enough to be next to Jesus, and he certainly wasn't good enough to deserve such bounty.

As Simon Peter hugged the ground, Jesus told him not to be afraid, because from that moment forward, Peter would be catching men instead of fish. Upon hearing this, Peter left everything behind—every last fish—and followed Jesus.

I once heard my pastor Bryan Counts say this about Peter's encounter with Jesus here:

> He likely recognizes that casting his nets is crazy and not by the book, but he still did it. He followed Jesus anyway. When Jesus overflows the boat with fish, Peter sees himself more clearly and believes he's not worthy. He left all the fish, and another sold it. Deciding to follow Jesus is a decision and a process.[1]

When we struggle to persevere on our own pathway, it's easy to be discouraged. But following Jesus on his specific back road for us isn't a onetime decision. To be sure, it's a process. Just as when we were young'uns and our parents' repeated guidance, discipline, and love helped bring us to adulthood, so the Lord's repeated guidance, discipline, and love do the same. There's no one-and-done in perseverance. Just a steady process, a one-foot-in-front-of-the-other choice after choice to stay on our individual back roads.

Following Jesus to where he wants us to belong isn't a onetime occurrence. It's a lifetime practice. He knows it's not easy, and he also knows it's worth it to keep going. *He's* worth it. God's faithful Word fuels us along the way.

> For you, O God, have tested us;
>   you have tried us as silver is tried.

> You brought us into the net;
>> you laid a crushing burden on our backs;
> you let men ride over our heads;
>> we went through fire and through water;
> *yet* you have brought us out to a place of abundance. (Ps. 66:10–12, emphasis mine)

Tough times on your back road will find you. The vines may climb, the brambles may poke, and the rains may beat you down. Keep going and persevere, dear one, for the difficulties come right before the *yet*. The Lord will bring you to your place of abundance.

That "playdate lunch" where nobody came? Heck yeah, it disappointed me. But I ended up calling some other moms who lived in the neighborhood, and we enjoyed a lovely time together eating and talking while the kids ran around like maniacs. This taught me that when my efforts at hospitality are a total failure, I can't let that "setback" be the end of it. Instead, I can let it spur me on in a different direction. Today, some fifteen-plus years later, I don't stay in touch with any of the moms from that moms' group. But I do stay in touch with several of those neighborhood moms, even though most of us don't live in the same neighborhood—or even the same state—anymore.

There's no getting around how traveling the back road way requires grit and perseverance. If we stop, we can start again. If we backtrack, we can come back. If we slow down, we can know slow movement is movement just the same. The resistance we feel is part of the journey. As we move forward, our spiritual formation is growing muscles. By the power of Jesus, God is making us more into who we are as he takes us to the people and places we belong. Have the patience and faith to go the crazy, it-doesn't-make-sense direction if God is the one calling you that direction. Your *yet* to abundance is coming. In the words of Oswald Chambers, "Every vision will be made real if we have patience."[2]

And perseverance.

traveling companion:
DANIEL

Talk about drama: the book of Daniel takes drama to all-new levels.

In chapter 10 of this Old Testament book, we find Daniel deeply troubled over a vision he received of impending war. His response to the vision? To fast and pray. After twenty-one days came and went, Daniel was greeted by an angel with a body made of mineral, a face that shone like lightning, eyes like torches, and arms and legs that gleamed like bronze (Dan. 10:6). The angel told Daniel,

> O Daniel, man greatly loved, understand the words that I speak to you, and stand upright, for now I have been sent to you. . . . Fear not, Daniel, for from the first day that you set your heart to understand and humbled yourself before your God, your words have been heard, and I have come because of your words. The prince of the kingdom of Persia withstood me twenty-one days, but Michael, one of the chief princes, came to help me, for I was left there with the kings of Persia, and came to make you understand what is to happen to your people in the latter days. (Dan. 10:11, 12–14)

While Daniel had prayed and fasted for three weeks with no direction from heaven, God's angels had answered the prayer immediately. A full-on battle raged in the heavenlies between God's angels and evil forces until Michael, a Navy SEAL of angels, entered the battle. Only then was the other angel released to give the response to Daniel directly.

I love how Pastor Max Lucado relates this encounter to us:

> Have your prayers been met with a silent sky? Have you prayed and heard nothing? Are you floundering in the land between an offered and answered prayer? If so, I beg you, don't give up. What the angel

said to Daniel, God says to you: "Since the first day that you set your mind to gain understanding and to humble yourself before your God, your words were heard" (Dan. 10:12 NIV). You have been heard in heaven. Angelic armies have been dispatched. Reinforcements have been rallied. God promises, "I will contend with him who contends with you" (Isa. 49:25, World English Bible).[3]

While it may take time for you to see the answers to your prayers about belonging, they are heard and dealt with immediately. God loves and cares so much for you that he sends the Special Forces of the angel armies to help you—in your minute and monumental concerns of wanting to fit in.

Another notable part of that passage is how Daniel was strengthened in the battle. Keep up the prayers, and you keep up your perseverance. Stay in conversation with God, and you stay your frustrations as you wait for your belonging place to make itself known.

~Belong Blessing~

As you tire on your own back road, may you feel and know the Lord gives you just what you need, moment by moment. As you're ever mindful of remaining in Christ and relaxing into God's plan for you, don't panic when that plan changes out of the blue. It may be hard now, but your *yet* is coming. Lay down every care and burden that is beyond your capability to handle. For at the end of yourself, you will find you needed only Jesus all along. He holds your cares, so you *will* persevere. May you remember the Lord works in all the crazy, and he will make sense of yours.

nineteen

Arriving
at Your Pathway's End

I sensed God telling me I had a choice to make: I could devote myself to becoming a strong and attractive tree that others would admire—"Look at those roots!" "Wow, look at all that fruit!"—or I could focus on planting a forest (that is, investing in others). God made it very clear to me what he would have me choose. And so I spend my days planting a forest.

Gary Thomas, *Sacred Parenting*

As a young mama living in New Mexico with her US Air Force husband, Rebecca enjoyed engaging with other moms and kids from various gatherings in her neighborhood and around town. She attended a MOPS (Mothers of Preschoolers) group at a large church and relished the benefits of participating in its established program. She also savored meaningful friendships within her neighborhood, and did what she could to attend to the needs of families within her church and her husband's workplace.

One day Rebecca lamented to her husband, Ryan, that there wasn't any on-base organization where moms could get together to encourage one another and get a break from their kiddos for an hour or two. Ryan listened, thought about what she said, then replied, "Well, if there's not a group like that there already, maybe you ought to build one."

Ryan's words only confirmed what Rebecca had heard from within. She loved the belonging place she had in her desert town, but she couldn't shake the feeling God was asking her to build a better belonging place for others too.

Armed with an open heart to welcome moms, the on-base chapel as a meeting venue, and neighborhood friends happy to help, Rebecca started a MOPS group on the military base where they lived. Within this group, moms met to hear from a speaker and then talk together for a couple hours while their young children stayed in childcare. It wasn't the flashiest, fanciest organization that ever met, but the women who came considered it a modern-day well, a place where they could convene and enjoy a good, long drink that watered their hearts and souls.

What I love about this part of Rebecca's story is she used what she knew and combined it with what she enjoyed to make the mom's group fit into her life. With a master's degree in early childhood education, Rebecca used her expertise to make the childcare room run as smoothly as possible. Rebecca also had a gift for planning and organizing events, so she put those talents to work as she served as coordinator of this MOPS group. Lastly, the gatherings gave her a small break from the demands of her own little ones. The belonging place Rebecca created at the end of her own pathway blessed her as it blessed others. Her belonging place was strengthened, and in building others up she was built up too.

• • •

Once we reach the end of our own personal back road, you and I will find it leads to a pathway toward our specific belonging place.

181

Who do you envision within that place? Who has God placed on your heart to welcome to its driveway, porch swing, or table? As you build others up there, you'll find yourself built up too. Give, and it will be given to you in return (Luke 6:38).

We know that because we are in Christ, we will always, *always* belong. "All that the Father gives me will come to me, and whoever comes to me I will never cast out" (John 6:37). Hallelujah and amen. Jesus will never leave us curbside because we didn't perform well enough, have the best ideas, or respond to every situation perfectly. He wants us beside him, and we have it on the authority of God's Word he'll never toss us away. He cherishes us.

Jesus doesn't only want us to know we belong on the inside and are enough as we are. He also asks us to know the best things await us when we welcome others in his name and help them know they belong too. "Where I am, there will my servant be also. If anyone serves me, the Father will honor him" (12:26). When we follow through and serve others, we are rewarded (Mark 9:41). One of those rewards? A more secure place of belonging. When we step out in faith to become a belong-maker of others, we see another way Christ shows us we belong more deeply.

In his own ministry, Jesus traveled a lot of roads preaching and healing and welcoming others. After he met with people, they were always better afterward than they were before. That's how I want to approach my place of belonging. Whatever is at the end of my pathway, no matter its size, are those spending time with me there better or worse after leaving than they were before they arrived?

This leads me to ask myself a few follow-up questions. Through words and actions, am I a belong-maker who builds others up? How can I create a belonging place that is a natural fit for my personality? One that, like Rebecca's, combines a bit of what I know with what I like to become something that works for me?

Jesus calls us lights that shine before others. Not so we'll look like we're all that and a bag of chips but so people will see us shining—building our belonging places for others—and will give God the credit for it (Matt. 5:16).

I want my life—including any belonging place of mine—to be a light that points others to Jesus. If we ignore Jesus's command to serve others, we bury our light in the ground instead of beaming it onto the world around us.

The way this comes to pass in each of our unique lives is as varied as the flowers along our path. Just because our friend over there volunteers every week at that nonprofit doesn't mean God is calling us to do the same. There are times when, in one way or another, our family, aka our priority people, demand more so we must give less to others. What we can do changes depending on our current season. For example, when I had small kids at home, I could more easily babysit other people's young kids on a regular basis because they folded right into mine. With three teens now, I can (and do) still babysit sometimes, but it's harder with my kids' full schedules that usually have us traveling in different directions. So now I'm more likely to make a meal for a friend or an acquaintance going through a difficult medical treatment. I help out once a month in the children's class at church during Sunday school. We welcome folks to our table for dinner. We sponsor and write letters to our Compassion children, something that has fit into our family well across multiple seasons. We do several other little things. And God turns our family's little things into big things that go the distance to welcome others in.

Whatever belonging place lies at the end of our pathway, I think this is key: we must make it something that folds into our life well. Let it fit within our family's personality, rhythms, and routines. That doesn't mean it won't be inconvenient from time to time. Most things worthwhile in life have an element of inconvenience and sacrifice. Still, many things that bless others take a minimal amount of effort yet give maximum rewards.

The baby in our family just started high school (How can this be?), and one thing that frustrates the ever-loving daylights out of me is the morning drop-off line. By 7:30 a.m., many of us parents are waiting in a ten-mile-long queue (give or take a mile) to drop off our teens.

The actual drop-off spot is a full semicircle, with the entrance to the school in its center. Ideally, parents dropping off their kids pull up all the way around the semicircle, so more parents behind them can let their kids out at a time. However, that isn't what happens. Over and over, parents pull up but stop in the middle of the semicircle—in front of the main door—to let their kids out. It seems many of them don't want their tender offspring walking an extra ten yards to the front door. Therefore the queue takes longer, and my eyeballs get plenty of practice rolling into orbit and back. If only more parents thought of the folks behind them and pulled all the way up in the drop-off zone, that small act would yield big rewards for the people behind them.

That's the way I want to approach the belonging places lying at the end of my own pathway. It's the smallest bit of extra effort that brings others in. It can be small and hidden, because the back road way is where we're seen less but sense our belonging more. It's the place where Jesus walks with us, assuring us his "Atta girl" is the only approval that's worth a hill of beans. It's a place where we practice self-compassion by viewing ourselves through the lens of Jesus rather than the lens of apology.

What's more, it's the place where we get to be ourselves, and be ourselves well. It's the place where change may come along and remove our belonging, yes, but really that change simply asks us to take a different, more refined road toward our belonging place. We don't need to panic but rather let that prepare us to be on the lookout for what God has in store.

Also, if the place at the end of our pathway doesn't feel like a place of belonging, it may just be it doesn't feel like a place of belonging *yet*. Don't despise those darker days, because growth still happens in the dark. It just happens in a downward direction. We're meant to belong, but first we must tend to our soul's soil as we rest and listen. And as we do that, we take care to look in all the right places to belong: in God's Word, in the company of his voice, and into the people near us with whom we already belong.

Do not despair; God most assuredly has a place for each of us at the end of our pathway. We can bravely walk to the table the Lord chooses for us. We can gain courage by speaking truth out loud to ourselves about how we do belong rather than listening to ourselves about how we don't.

Remember, when we share our hard stuff, we invite others to do the same as we all move closer to our own place of belonging. We can make a regular practice of encouraging others—through our hard stuff and through their accomplishments. But we don't dare share with just anyone, and we don't fret if we find ourselves outside of where we used to be in. Sometimes being on the outside of a certain group or place is the healthiest place to be.

If we sense the Lord calling us beyond our fences and into the lives of people outside our usual stomping grounds, then we can hurdle those perceived barriers and make an introduction. We may find ourselves smack-dab in the middle of a profound place of belonging that is better than we could ever fathom.

And when we've done all the "right" things and still struggle to find our place and people, we don't lose hope. Following Jesus to our belonging place isn't a onetime occurrence. It's a lifelong practice. He kept walking his own back roads throughout his entire life, and he won't neglect us as we do the same. We can hold his hand through prayer and let him see us to the place and people awaiting us at the end of our pathway.

• • •

When my family and I lived in Dayton, Ohio, we attended a beautiful little church called Emmanuel Lutheran. A sign stood at attention outside both parking lot exits of this church: "You are now entering the mission field." It was a simple yet powerful reminder that once we left the church parking lot, we arrived at our place of neighborly work. Whether we live in our church's own neighborhood or want to help a neighborhood across the globe, we can do so with the confidence that no gesture is too small, unimportant, or off-mission.

For those of us who are in Christ, we each bear a responsibility to live out the gospel through the grace and privilege of good works within our chosen neighborhoods. Each of us also bears a responsibility to build others up in their belonging place. And to welcome them into ours.

Scripture reaffirms for us that, in its truest form, our belonging place is not something to achieve but something to receive. "I took the burdens off your backs; I let you put down your loads of bricks" (Ps. 81:6 GNT). We don't have to work to belong to Christ because Jesus already did the work to bring us in.

He doesn't ask us to wear ourselves plumb out, to walk hunched over from carrying what isn't ours to carry. He doesn't ask us to live bone-dry from being everything to everyone. He asks each of us to simply mind our own place at the end of the pathway, because showing up there adds that glorious spark no one else can replicate.

In the end, the choice is ours: Do we want to be the car that stops short in the drop-off line, because we don't want ourselves or our people to be inconvenienced in the least? Or do we want to expend a little effort to make room for someone else? To bring another in? To be a small sign pointing the way to his or her belonging place?

First and foremost, you, dear one, "belong to another, to him who has been raised from the dead, in order that we may bear fruit for God" (Rom. 7:4). Second, might I welcome you to sit on my porch swing here and tell me a bit of your story? May I remind you that, as long as your back road encourages you to remain in Christ and relax into God's plan for you today, then you're going the right way?

One day, you'll have every belonging-hole filled so that you're wholly you and wholly loved alongside our Savior in heaven. Today, the Lord will see you through your back road. Jesus walks with you, curious to have you share your whole story with him too. Yes, he already knows it, but sharing it is a good way for you to remain close to him.

The porch swing rocks back and forth for us, and it's the rhythm of a future that looks a whole lot like freedom to live and love as ourselves.

Because you and I belong.
May we remain and relax . . . and rejoice.

traveling companion :
BEAUTIFUL YOU

Dear reader, it's been my joy and privilege to be your back road traveling companion as you walk to the specific place of belonging God has picked out for you. I urge you to be alert and expectant; your own belonging place is at the end of your pathway. Whether you want to sponsor a Compassion child, make a monthly donation to a nonprofit, start a nonprofit, volunteer at a downtown kitchen, take a meal to a mom who just had a baby, start your own group that meets for mutual encouragement, become a foster parent, or something totally different, know you're standing in the right place whenever you move to bring another in.

One word of caution: don't let anyone else's belonging place determine your own. Let God's direction do that for you. He knows you through and through, and he'll make a way for you to combine what you know and what you enjoy to do what fits within your life. Rest in knowing that when you remain in Christ and relax into God's plans for you, you'll have a heart willing and happy to welcome another in.

~ *Belong Blessing* ~

As you keep your eyes and heart open to see how, where, and who God asks you to welcome in, may you feel peace over anxiety. Let go of any and all statements including the word *should*, and instead try this simple phrase:

187

Make your way for me, Lord. God always picks up what impossible lays down. May you let him take the burden from your shoulders. May you be comfortable being seen less, because this is how you know your belonging more. Today and every day, may you know the calming freedom that comes with remaining in Christ and relaxing into God's role for you. You're so beloved.

Helpful Resources

THE FOLLOWING LIST OF RESOURCES, which I've compiled with the help of generous readers, are some favorite tools we can use to receive regular biblical encouragement.

- You Version (www.youversion.com) has products to help experience the Bible daily, like a Bible app and Bible app for kids.
- (in)courage (www.incourage.me), the DaySpring blog, offers daily devotionals.
- Bible.Is (www.bible.is) is a resource for reading and studying God's Word, listening to the Bible in hundreds of languages, and seeing Scripture come to life through film integration.
- Olive Tree Bible Software (www.olivetree.com) offers a Bible app providing access to Scripture as well as devotionals.
- MOPS (www.mops.org) is a Christian organization supporting mothers of preschoolers.
- Bible Study Fellowship (www.bsfinternational.org) is an organization committed to Christ that provides global, in-depth Bible classes to magnify God and mature his people into deeper relationships with him.
- Brownicity (www.brownicity.com) offers resources that foster racial healing.

- Arise Ministries (www.ariseministries.net) empowers single moms to create healthy homes through Bible studies and other resources.

- Bible Hub (www.biblehub.com) facilitates the study of Scripture, with tools to compare and contrast the same verse in multiple translations and study biblical commentaries.

- Blue Letter Bible (www.blueletterbible.org) provides tools to study Scripture as well as a free online reference library.

- Daily Audio Bible (www.dailyaudiobible.com) is an app that empowers and equips readers to include Scripture in their daily rhythms, with the commitment of guiding Christians worldwide into an intimate familiarity and friendship with the Bible.

- The Bible (www.bible.com) is an app that lets users highlight and bookmark passages from over twelve thousand versions of the Bible in over nine hundred languages, with audio Bibles available as well.

- She Reads Truth (www.shereadstruth.com) is an app that makes it easy for women of God to be in the Word every day, with fifteen available Bible reading plans. Join the worldwide community of women devoted to reading the Bible together daily.

- Bible Gateway (www.biblegateway.com) is designed to encourage easy reading, listening, studying, searching, and sharing of the Bible in many versions and translations. It also offers Bible-focused news and opportunities to delve deeper into the Word through online courses.

- Sara Hagerty's monthly printables (www.sarahagerty.net /printables/) include a daily verse and truth about that verse, and are an excellent launching pad for writing out the verse and journaling/praying about it.

- First 5 (www.proverbs31.org/study/first-5) is an app from Proverbs 31 Ministries.

The following organizations are examples of those that my family and my readers support in an effort to bring others in. Feel free to send me your own favorite resources via the contact page at www.kristenstrong.com.

- Mercy House Global (www.mercyhouseglobal.org) rescues pregnant teen girls in Kenya and empowers them through faith and fair trade product development. They also help sixty-one nonprofits in thirty-one countries sell artisan-made products.
- A21 Campaign (www.a21.org) is a nonprofit organization committed to eradicating human trafficking through awareness, intervention, and aftercare. The men and women involved with A21 are abolitionists of the twenty-first century.
- Preemptive Love (www.preemptivelove.org) is a coalition stretching across Iraq, Syria, and the United States that provides relief for war-torn families and jobs for refugees.
- Folds of Honor (www.foldsofhonor.org) is a nonprofit organization that works to provide educational opportunities via financial aid to families of fallen or wounded American soldiers.
- Compassion International (www.compassion.com) is a child-advocacy ministry that joins compassionate people with those suffering from poverty. It releases children from spiritual, economic, social, and physical poverty.
- The Shop Forward (www.theshopforward.com) supports charities by selling items attached to a cause. Since opening in 2014, they've raised close to three million dollars.
- World Vision (www.worldvision.org) is an international Christian humanitarian organization that partners with children, families, and their communities to empower people out of poverty.
- Mercy Ships (www.mercyships.org) helps provide lifesaving surgeries and care for people who live where medical resources

are nearly nonexistent, and it's done from the world's biggest civilian hospital ship.

- Joni and Friends (www.joniandfriends.org) is an organization that communicates the gospel and accelerates Christian ministry to the disabled community.

- Live Fashionable (www.livefashionable.com) is a lifestyle brand focused on ending generational poverty by providing economic opportunity for women.

- The Jason Foundation (www.thejasonfoundation.com) is dedicated to preventing youth suicide through programs that educate and provide awareness to youth, educators, and parents. They also offer resources that help identify and assist at-risk youth.

- Moms in Prayer (www.momsinprayer.org) is a worldwide community of moms praying for their children and schools in all fifty states and in over 140 countries.

- The Voice of the Martyrs, or VOM (www.persecution.com), is a nonprofit, interdenominational Christian mission organization providing practical and spiritual assistance to persecuted families worldwide.

- KLOVE radio (www.klove.com) is a media station that encourages people to have a meaningful relationship with Christ.

- Morning Star Foundation (www.morningstar.foundation) provides help to needy children with severe heart disease in China and Uganda. Their projects include a foster home for orphans in China with complicated heart defects.

- Lifeline Children Services (www.lifelinechild.org) has a mission to equip the body of Christ to manifest the gospel to vulnerable children.

- Navigators (www.navigators.org) is an international, interdenominational Christian ministry that strives to know Christ and help others to do the same. They offer mentoring and discipling programs as well as resources that equip Christ-followers to impact people around them for God's glory.

- Johnny Mac Soldiers Fund (www.johnnymac.org) honors our military's sacrifice and service by providing scholarships to veterans and military family members, particularly children of our nation's fallen and disabled.

IN A CRISIS?

If you or someone you love may be suicidal, please contact the Suicide Prevention Hotline at 1-800-273-8255.

Other helpful resources for those in crisis:

- Alive to Thrive (www.alivetothrive.focusonthefamily.com)
- Mercy Multiplied (www.mercymultiplied.com)
- To Write Love on Her Arms (www.twloha.com)

To find a Christian counselor in your area, check into www.ecounseling.com, set up by the American Association of Christian Counselors. This site allows you to put in your zip code to find a counselor near you.

For those who've lost someone to suicide, consider the book *Grieving a Suicide: A Loved One's Search for Comfort, Answers, and Hope* by Albert Y. Hsu.

Scriptures That Affirm You Belong

But Jesus called them to him, saying, "Let the children come to me, and do not hinder them, for to such belongs the kingdom of God." (Luke 18:16)

> Make sure no outsider who now follows GOD
>   ever has occasion to say, "God put me in second-class.
>   I don't really belong."
> And make sure no physically mutilated person
>   is ever made to think, "I'm damaged goods.
>   I don't really belong." (Isa. 56:2–3 Message)

> And a highway shall be there,
>   and it shall be called the Way of Holiness;
> the unclean shall not pass over it.
>   It shall belong to those who walk on the way;
>   even if they are fools, they shall not go astray. (Isa. 35:8)

Then I will gather the remnant of my flock out of all the countries where I have driven them, and I will bring them back to their fold, and they shall be fruitful and multiply. I will set shepherds over them who will care for them, and they shall fear no more, nor be dismayed, neither shall any be missing, declares the LORD. (Jer. 23:3–4)

As sure as I'm the living God . . . Every soul—man, woman, child— belongs to me, parent and child alike. (Ezek. 18:4 Message)

The physical part of you is not some piece of property belonging to the spiritual part of you. God owns the whole works. So let people see God in and through your body. (1 Cor. 6:19–20 Message)

Therefore, brothers, since we have confidence to enter the holy places by the blood of Jesus, by the new and living way that he opened for us through the curtain, that is, through his flesh, and since we have a great priest over the house of God, let us draw near with a true heart in full assurance of faith, with our hearts sprinkled clean from an evil conscience and our bodies washed with pure water. (Heb. 10:19–22)

The secret things belong to the LORD our God, but the things that are revealed belong to us and to our children forever, that we may do all the words of this law. (Deut. 29:29)

Let us then with confidence draw near to the throne of grace, that we may receive mercy and find grace to help in time of need. (Heb. 4:16)

And he brought us out from there, that he might bring us in and give us the land that he swore to give to our fathers. (Deut. 6:23)

> They feast on the abundance of your house;
> > you give them drink from the river of your delights. (Ps. 36:8)

> Your steadfast love, O LORD, extends to the heavens,
> > your faithfulness to the clouds. (Ps. 36:5)

> You crown the year with your bounty;
> > your wagon tracks overflow with abundance. (Ps. 65:11)

This I know, that God is for me. (Ps. 56:9)

Nevertheless, I am continually with you;
    you hold my right hand.
You guide me with your counsel,
    and afterward you will receive me to glory. (Ps.
      73:23–24)

Relax and rest.
    GOD has showered you with blessings.
    Soul, you've been rescued from death;
    Eye, you've been rescued from tears;
    And you, Foot, were kept from stumbling. (Ps. 116:7–8
      Message)

Every valley shall be lifted up,
    and every mountain and hill be made low;
the uneven ground shall become level,
    and the rough places a plain.
And the glory of the LORD shall be revealed,
    and all flesh shall see it together,
      for the mouth of the LORD has spoken. (Isa. 40:4–5)

All that the Father gives me will come to me, and whoever comes to me I will never cast out. (John 6:37)

He went on his way through towns and villages, teaching and journeying toward Jerusalem. And someone said to him, "Lord, will those who are saved be few?" And he said to them, "Strive to enter through the narrow door." (Luke 13:22–24)

Therefore welcome one another as Christ has welcomed you, for the glory of God. (Rom. 15:7)

But our citizenship is in heaven, and from it we await a Savior, the Lord Jesus Christ. (Phil. 3:20)

Notes

Introduction

1. Deborah Moggach, "Pride and Prejudice," *Internet Movie Script Database*, accessed December 10, 2018, http://www.imsdb.com/scripts/Pride-and-Prejudice .html.

Chapter 1 Sitting Out

1. Maggie Fox, "Suicide Rates Are up 30 Percent Since 1999, CDC Says," *NBC News*, June 7, 2018, https://www.nbcnews.com/health/health-news/suicide-rates -are-30-percent-1999-cdc-says-n880926.

2. Blair Miller, "El Paso County's High among Adults, Teens Highlighted in Newsweek Report," *The Denver Channel*, October 19, 2016, https://www.thedenver channel.com/news/local-news/el-paso-countys-high-suicide-rates-among-adults -teens-highlighted-in-newsweek-report.

3. Lauren Fisher et al., "From the Outside Looking In: Sense of Belonging, Depression, and Suicide Risk," *Psychiatry* 78 (2015): 29–41.

4. George Gordon Coulton, *From St. Francis to Dante* (London: David Nutt, 1907), 97.

Chapter 2 Traveling Extremes

1. Vince Hoppe, "We Become What We Worship," Village Seven Presbyterian Church, January 7, 2018, http://www.v7pc.org/pages/page.asp?page_id=402550 &programId=264355.

2. Kristen Hatton, "Behind the Screens of the Selfie World of Teens," *By Faith* 4, no. 58 (2017): 40.

3. Jean M. Twenge, "Have Smartphones Destroyed a Generation?" *The Atlantic*, September 2017, https://www.theatlantic.com/magazine/archive/2017/09/has -the-smartphone-destroyed-a-generation/534198/.

4. Katherine Hobson, "Feeling Lonely? Too Much Time on Social Media May Be Why," *NPR*, March 6, 2017, https://www.npr.org/sections/health-shots/2017/03/06/518362255/feeling-lonely-too-much-time-on-social-media-may-be-why.

Chapter 3 Getting You

1. Beth Moore, *The Quest: An Excursion Toward Intimacy with God* (Nashville: Lifeway, 2018), 86.

2. Shelly Miller, "Why Wandering Might Be Your Best Work," *Shelly Miller Writer* (blog), April 25, 2018, http://shellymillerwriter.com/2018/04/25/wandering-might-best-work/.

3. Dr. Thomas Brisco, cartographer, *Palestine in the Time of Jesus* (Nashville: Broadman & Holman, 2003).

4. Alli's story taken from personal conversations and emails with the author. Used by permission.

5. Moore, *The Quest*, 86.

6. Holley Gerth, *Fiercehearted: Live Fully, Love Bravely* (Grand Rapids: Revell, 2017), 56.

7. Holley Gerth, "When God Changes Your Plans: An Infertility Update," *Holley Gerth* (blog), August 23, 2013, https://holleygerth.com/when-god-changes-your-plans-an-infertility-update/.

8. Holley's story taken from personal conversations with the author. Used by permission.

9. Gerth, *Fiercehearted*, 56.

10. This part of Holley's story also taken from personal conversations with the author. Used by permission.

Chapter 4 Extending Kindness to Yourself

1. Leeana Tankersley, "When It's Time to Stop Apologizing for Yourself," *Leeana Tankersley* (blog), February 18, 2016, https://www.leeanatankersley.com/when-its-time-to-stop-apologizing-for-yourself/.

Chapter 5 Singing Loudly

1. Søren Kierkegaard, *Søren Kierkegaard's Journals and Papers: Autobiographical, 1829–1848*, vol. 5, ed. and trans. by Howard V. Hong and Edna H. Hong with Gregor Malantschuk (Bloomington: Indiana University Press, 1978), 443.

2. Matthew Henry, *Matthew Henry's Commentary on the Whole Bible (Complete)*, accessed November 8, 2018, https://www.biblestudytools.com/commentaries/matthew-henry-complete/genesis/29.html.

3. D. A. Carson, R. T. France, J. A. Motyer, and G. J. Wenham, *New Bible Commentary: 21st Century Edition* (Downers Grove, IL: InterVarsity Press, 2004), 80, emphasis in original.

4. Liz Curtis Higgs, "Leah," *Word by Word* (podcast), 22:20 mark, https://www.lizcurtishiggs.com/word-by-word-leah/.

5. Liz Curtis Higgs, "Leah," *Word by Word* (podcast), 23:10 mark, https://www .lizcurtishiggs.com/word-by-word-leah/.

Chapter 6 Belonging to Change

1. Connie's story taken from personal conversations with the author. Used by permission.

Chapter 7 Growing in the Dark

1. Michael Snyder, "What Do Tree Roots Do in Winter?" *Northern Woodlands*, December 1, 2007, https://northernwoodlands.org/articles/article/what_do _tree_roots_do_in_winter.
2. "Barnes' Notes: Luke 24," Bible Hub, accessed December 11, 2018, https:// biblehub.com/commentaries/barnes/luke/24.htm.
3. Richard Louv, *Last Child in the Woods: Saving Our Children from Nature-Deficit Disorder* (Chapel Hill, NC: Algonquin Books, 2008), 51.
4. Gayle Boss, *All Creation Waits: The Advent Mystery of New Beginnings* (Brewster, MA: Paraclete Press, 2016), 11.
5. Boss, *All Creation Waits*, 11.
6. Jules Evans, "What's the Difference between Bird Songs and Bird Calls?" *Bay Nature*, July 1, 2001, https://baynature.org/article/whats-the-difference-between -bird-songs-and-bird-calls/.
7. Bob Sundstrom, "Singer's Brain Changes with the Seasons," *BirdNote*, March 2015/2018, https://www.birdnote.org/show/singers-brain-changes-seasons.
8. Kristen Strong, "When You Need Friends but Have a Hard Time Finding Them," (in)courage, February 1, 2012, https://www.incourage.me/2012/02/when -you-need-friends-but-have-a-hard-time-finding-them.html. Comment by Aundrea used by permission.

Chapter 8 Eating Well

1. Kelli Campbell, "Semper Fi," *Sealy News*, November 6, 2017, http://www .sealynews.com/stories/semper-fi,77103.
2. Kelli's story taken from personal conversations and emails with the author. Used by permission.
3. Campbell, "Semper Fi."
4. Kristen Strong, "When the Worst Happens (And How You Can Give the Best Help)," (in)courage, May 30, 2016, https://www.incourage.me/2016/05/when-the -worst-happens-and-how-you-can-give-the-best-help.html.

Chapter 9 Looking in the Quiet

1. Chip and Joanna Gaines, *The Magnolia Story* (Nashville: Thomas Nelson, 2016), 82.
2. "The Gathering Testimony: Joanna Gaines," Vimeo video, 4:28, posted by Antioch Community Church, 2015, https://vimeo.com/125510141.

3. Gary Thomas, *Sacred Parenting: How Raising Children Shapes Our Souls* (Grand Rapids: Zondervan, 2009), 111.

Chapter 10 Looking into Your People

1. Rebecca McClanahan, *Word Painting: The Fine Art of Writing Descriptively* (Cincinnati: Writer's Digest Books, 2014), 14.
2. Michelle's story taken from personal conversations with the author. Used by permission.

Chapter 11 Growing Up and Out

1. Gretchen Rubin, "Podcast 110: A Very Special Episode on a Major Happiness Stumbling Block—Are You Lonely?" *Happier with Gretchen Rubin* (podcast), March 29, 2017, 29:00 mark, https://gretchenrubin.com/podcast-episode/podcast-110-lonely.
2. Johann Hari, "Is Everything You Think You Know about Depression Wrong?" *The Guardian*, January 7, 2018, https://www.theguardian.com/society/2018/jan/07/is-everything-you-think-you-know-about-depression-wrong-johann-hari-lost-connections?CMP=share_btn_tw.
3. Hari, "Is Everything You Think You Know about Depression Wrong?"
4. Emmy's story taken from personal conversations with the author. Used by permission.

Chapter 12 Talking More, Listening Less

1. Ruth Chou Simons, Instagram caption, June 4, 2018, https://www.instagram.com/p/BjoKmeFg9nM/?taken-by=gracelaced.
2. Ruth Chou Simons, Instagram caption, May 15, 2018, https://www.instagram.com/p/BizOSQpAap0/?taken-by=gracelaced.
3. Sruthi, "Does Reading Out Loud Cause You to Remember Things Better?" *Brainscape* (blog), May 14, 2017, https://www.brainscape.com/blog/2011/10/reading-out-loud-remember/.
4. Charles Spurgeon, *Morning and Evening: A New Edition of the Classic Devotional Based on the Holy Bible, English Standard Version*, revised and updated by Alistair Begg (Wheaton: Crossway, 2003), September 13.
5. Beth Moore, *The Patriarchs: Encountering the God of Abraham, Isaac, and Jacob* (Nashville: Lifeway, 2005), 36.
6. Moore, *Patriarchs*, 39.

Chapter 13 Helping the Hard (but Worth It) Way

1. Amanda Enayati, "The Importance of Belonging," *CNN*, June 1, 2012, http://www.cnn.com/2012/06/01/health/enayati-importance-of-belonging/index.html.
2. Brené Brown, *Daring Greatly: How the Courage to Be Vulnerable Transforms the Way We Live, Love, Parent, and Lead* (New York: Avery, 2015), Kindle loc. 145.

3. Lisa-Jo Baker, "Being Brave Enough to Be Unfine," *Lisa-Jo Baker* (blog), March 12, 2013, http://lisajobaker.com/2013/03/being-brave-enough-to-be-un-fine/.

Chapter 14 Belonging Isn't for You

1. Justin Taylor, "What Does the Tabernacle Symbolize?" The Gospel Coalition, October 24, 2011, https://www.thegospelcoalition.org/blogs/justin-taylor/what -does-the-tabernacle-symbolize/.

2. Taylor, "What Does the Tabernacle Symbolize?"

3. NIV study notes, "Exodus 25:30," *NIV Study Bible* (Grand Rapids: Zondervan, 2002), 125.

4. Chelsea's story taken from personal conversations with the author. Used by permission.

Chapter 15 Speaking Up and Out

1. Ann Voskamp, "10 Point Manifesto for Joyful Parenting," *Ann Voskamp* (blog), accessed March 20, 2019, https://annvoskamp.com/10-points-of-joyful-parenting -printable/.

Chapter 16 Being Belong-Makers

1. Dietrich Bonhoeffer, *Watch for the Light: Readings for Advent and Christmas* (Walden, NY: Plough Publishing, 2014), December 21.

Chapter 17 Going There Anyway

1. Kate Andersen Brower, *First Women: The Grace and Power of America's Modern First Ladies* (New York: HarperCollins, 2017), 65–66.

2. Brower, *First Women*, 65.

Chapter 18 Persevering on the Path

1. Bryan Counts, taken from the author's Sunday school notes, July 22, 2018.

2. Oswald Chambers, *My Utmost for His Highest* (Uhrichsville, OH: Barbour, 1963), July 7.

3. Max Lucado, *Anxious for Nothing: Finding Calm in a Chaotic World* (Nashville: Thomas Nelson, 2017), 110.

Kristen Strong, author of *Girl Meets Change*, writes as a friend offering meaningful encouragement for each season of life so you can see it with more hope and less worry. She and her US Air Force veteran husband, David, have three children. Together this military family zigzagged across the country (and one ocean) several times before settling in Colorado Springs, Colorado. You can find her at kristenstrong.com, DaySpring's (in)courage, and on Instagram @kristenstrong.

Connect with Kristen

 kristenstrong

 Chasing Blue Skies

 Kristen_Strong

 Kristen Strong